ROCK GUITAR

ROCK GUITAR

Revised Edition

Edited By Helen Casabona

The Guitar Player Basic Library

From the editors of Guitar Player magazine.

Hal Leonard Publishing Corporation

7777 West Bluemound Road P.O. Box 13819 Milwaukee, WI 53213

GPI BOOKS

Director
Alan Rinzler

Editor: Rock Guitar Revised Edition
Helen Casabona

Art Director
Paul Haggard

General Manager
Judie Eremo

Art Assistant
Robert Stockwell, Jr.

Assistant
Marjean Wall

GPI PUBLICATIONS

President/Publisher
Jim Crockett

Executive Vice President
Don Menn

Corporate Art Director
Wales Christian Ledgerwood

Editor: Guitar Player
Tom Wheeler

Editor: Frets
Phil Hood

Production
Cheryl Matthews (Director)
Joyce Phillips (Assistant Director)
Andrew Gordon, Gail M. Hall, Joe Verri

Typesetting
Leslie K. Bartz (Director)
Pat Gates, June Ramirez

Order Processing
Rekha Shah
Lynne Whitlach

Photo Credits
Cover: Paul Haggard

Guitar courtesy of Carvin Musical Instruments

Anastasia Pantsios/Kaleyediscope: 36.
Paul Haggard: 1, 110.
Paul Natkin/Photo Reserve: vi.
Deborah Roth: 56 (all photos), 57, 101, 102 (all photos).
Jon Sievert: 43 (all photos), 44 (all photos), 45 (all photos), 46 (all photos), 47 (all photos), 63.
Robert Stockwell Jr.: 21, 40 (all photos), 41 (top left, top right, middle), 93, 100, (all photos), 104 (all photos).
Neil Zlozower: 15 (all photos), 17, 18, 19, 118.

Album Covers on pages 112-117 courtesy of the following:

Duane Eddy, Have "Twangy" Guitar, Will Travel; The Rolling Stones, Beggars Banquet; and *The Allman Brothers Band At Filmore East* courtesy Big Al's Record Barn, Santa Clara, Ca.

The Ventures, Walk, Don't Run; Jimi Hendrix Experience, Are You Experienced; and *Led Zeppelin II* courtesy Paul Haggard.

Chuck Berry, The Great Twenty-Eight and *The Who, Live At Leeds* courtesy Gretchen Horton.

Derek And The Dominos, Layla; Steely Dan, The Royal Scam; Dixie Dregs, What If; and *The Police, Ghost In The Machine* courtesy Jake Hunter.

Ricky Nelson, Ricky Nelson courtesy Tom Wheeler.

Jeff Beck, Blow By Blow and *The Yardbirds, Having A Rave Up With The Yardbirds* courtesy Epic Records.

ISBN: 088188-908-3

Contents

Introduction

GPI Publications launched the *Guitar Player Basic Library* to preserve some of the finest columns of information, inspiration, and advice written by working professional musicians. This library consists of a series of definitive volumes containing collections of redesigned and reprinted articles, many of which are otherwise unavailable because the original issues are out of print.

The first edition of *Rock Guitar*, a volume in this library, was designed as a comprehensive, practical introduction to the technique and art of playing rock guitar. This revised edition carries on the tradition, retaining some of the otherwise unavailable material from its predecessor while featuring over 70 new pages of articles, columns, musical examples, and solo transcriptions from recent issues of *Guitar Player* magazine. Such phenomenal players, teachers, and stars as Lee Ritenour, Larry Coryell, Arlen Roth, Rik Emmett, Eddie Van Halen, Steve Vai, Brad Gillis, Steve Morse, and many others will take you from the art of playing rhythm to mastering electric guitar techniques, playing lead, and even playing slide guitar. Examined and transcribed is the music of such outstanding rock performers as Eric Clapton, Steve Vai, George Lynch, Duane Allman, and Randy Rhoads.

Although *Rock Guitar* is an introduction to playing rock guitar, the wealth of information and skills to be acquired from within these pages will challenge the aspiring hobbiest or professional of any ability for years to come.

Helen Casabona

Chapter 1:
Getting Started

Tuning Your Guitar

Guitar Player, July 1984.

There's a frequent sit-com that happens at our store: A player lays a fine guitar on the counter and informs me that the frets are in the wrong place! The first-position C chord sounds well in tune, but the seventh-position E major chord is all out. He's right. But chances are, it is not because of the frets. It is a pure and simple case of the guitar not being tuned properly. It's not always a good idea to tell a person who's been playing for many years that he or she doesn't know how to tune a guitar, so I restrain myself and suggest that the *strings* are faulty. I sell that person a new set of the same strings, put them on, stretch them out, and tune the instrument correctly. The usual cheerful comment I hear: "I can't believe how bad those strings were!"

Very few days pass that I'm not confronted by a guitarist frustrated by problems directly related to stringing and tuning. Another frequent complaint is that "the keys are slipping." The chances of even the cheapest worm-gear tuners slipping is extremely remote. On checking, the problem invariably turns out to be the way the strings were put on—that is, there are open loops around the key posts, not enough turns around them to lock the strings, or a lack of understanding of the worm gear itself. If there are open loops around the post, or if an unwrapped (plain) string isn't wrapped around the post a sufficient number of times, a little tug on the string will usually cause it to loosen.

Tuning To Pitch

If the player has the bad habit of tuning too high and then lowering the string to pitch and leaving the key as is, there will be just enough space—perhaps only thousandths of an inch—left in the worm gear to allow the string to go flat when picked. The answer? When tuning lower, *always* tune at least a half-step *below* the desired pitch: stretch the string to make sure there is no slack left in the gear, and then tune *up* to the desired pitch. You can prove the effectiveness of this very easily by tuning the high E string sharp, and then backing off until the pitch is the same as the E at the 5th fret on the B string. Next give a firm tug on the first string, and you'll be surprised at how flat it is. Now reverse the procedure: Tune the E string sharp and compare its pitch with the fretted E on the second string. Then tune the E string approximately a half-step lower than the fingered E, stretch the string firmly, and tune up to the desired pitch. If you tug on the string, you'll notice how much better it stays at pitch. The bottom line? Always tune *up* to pitch.

Figure 1.

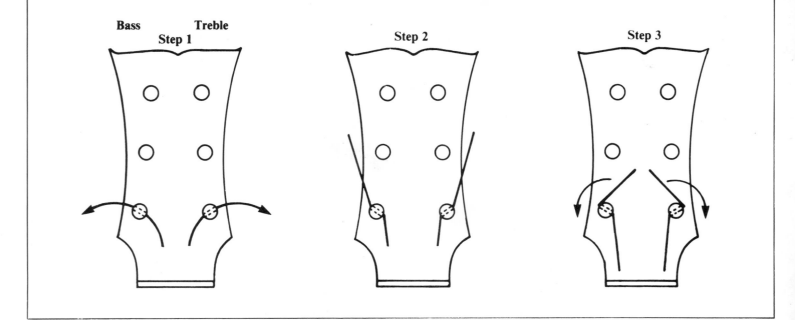

Correct Stringing Technique

The variations in stringing methods are a never-ending source of amazement. Some folks feel that you have to tie knots in the strings around the post. Others think that you have to run the strings through the posthole as many times as the string's diameter allows, while still others believe that you should use every inch of the string—ending up with an unstable blob of wire wrapped around the post. But excess windings can cause the string to twist; if twisted enough, the string may vibrate inconsistently and give a false pitch. The whole idea is to string in a way that facilitates both the initial installation as well as changing. I often spend a good half-hour of wasted time at the workbench just removing the old strings that were put on wrong. Can you imagine the look on the customer's face if I were to charge the same hourly rate as a plumber?

One of the most expeditious and stable methods of stringing is shown in Figure 1. After you put the string through the posthole, bend it sharply to lock it to the post right from the start. You should have approximately three turns for each wrapped string, and about twice as many on the unwrapped strings. This, plus a generous amount of stretching, results in a very stable string condition. Winding the remainder of the loose string toward the bottom of the post greatly reduces leverage/torque pressure on the post, therefore reducing excess gear wear.

Take the time to look at the pin block of a piano. The makers of even the cheapest pianos realize one thing above all else: The strings have to be put on correctly, or those manufacturers will be out of business—period. If the strings aren't correctly installed, there is no way the instrument will hold a tuning long enough to get it off the showroom floor. For the concerned player, the guitar is in exactly the same boat. The photos in Figures 2 and 3 show both neat and sloppy stringing techniques.

Figure 2.

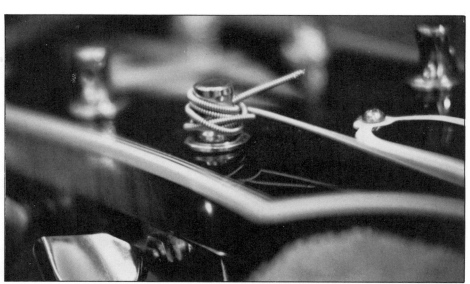

Figure 3.

String Gauges

Good intonation means that we can get chords to sound in tune all the way up and down the neck, and string gauges can greatly affect the quality of intonation. I can't think of one brand of strings on the market today that isn't of good quality. For solidbody guitars using string sets with an unwrapped G string, I have found that the following gauges give us the best results when setting up the intonation: .010, .013, .017, .026, .036, .046. It has been my experience that extra-light and especially super-light strings in particular are all but impossible to set up for good intonation.

As for the acoustic-body electrics and straight acoustic guitars, most players use string sets with wrapped G strings (as well they should), which greatly minimize intonation problems. Plain third strings are often the main source of faulty intonation. These strings have a tendency to sound sharp, and if they are too light, bridge saddle adjustment cannot compensate for them. On a well-adjusted bridge, the saddle insert for a plain G string is invariably located closer to the rear of the bridge than the other inserts. This is why I do not recommend using plain thirds on acoustic arch-top and flat-top guitars with slanted bridge saddles that cannot be adjusted for individual strings.

On arch-top and flat-top acoustics, the second string can also cause an intonation propblem. If the B string is too heavy, it reacts in the same way as the plain third string—that is, it has a tendency to go sharp in the upper register. Back in the days of big band rhythm guitar, very heavy strings were used. As a result, the bridge saddles had to be notched out to the rear under the second string to help correct the intonation. With the string gauges used by most players of today's acoustic-body guitars, this notched-out bridge saddle is a problem causing the second string to fret flat in the upper register. Most modern manufacturers use an unnotched, slanted bridge saddle that gives excellent intonation with the approximate string gauges recommended here: .012, .016, .024 (wound), .032, .042, .054.

For guitars with fixed bridges, such as classical and folk models, trying different gauges is usually the only solution to intonation problems. Some classical guitar builders cut an offset to the rear under the third string to help compensate for the inherent sharp qualities of the unwrapped nylon third string.

Setting Intonation

If you want to play in tune, good intonation is a must. There is no deep, dark secret to this: Setting intonation can be done adequately by most players without the use of a strobe tuner or gifted musical ears. I will always remember the beautiful, sparkling sound of the pianos when I was doing studio work in New York City. Even to this day, most of the outstanding piano tuners I know carry their tuning kits in one coat pocket; a tuning fork, a strip of felt, a rubber wedge, and a tuning hammer. Through years of experience, they have trained their ears to be able to set up a tempered scale that's the most accurate for a particular instrument. I believe the same is true for guitars: Each one is a little different in its acoustic response—even the solid bodies.

First-String Intonation

Some people set the bridge or insert placement by aligning the pitch of the fretted E at the 12th fret to the harmonic E at the 12th fret. This alone is okay, but if you really want to nail it down, adjust it so that the fingered B at the 19th fret on the first string has the same pitch as the harmonic B at the 19th fret; now you can be sure that the bridge/insert placement for the first string is correct. Rule: If the fretted note is sharp compared to the harmonic, move the bridge/insert *back*, increasing the string length. If the fretted note is flat compared to the harmonic, move the bridge/insert *forward*, decreasing the string length. For arch-top guitars with movable bridges and slanted saddles, this will be the only bridge adjustment you should make. If intonation problems exist when you are going through the sequence illustrated here, your only solution may be to try different string gauges. The base of the bridge should *not* be canted.

Using harmonics to adjust the tuning or intonation of your guitar would be okay if you played *only* harmonics all the time. This is not the way it is, and the only realistic method is to set the intonation to fretted notes up the neck—which is the way you play, for the most part.

Intonating The Other Strings

Start by tuning the second string so that the pitch of the fretted E (5th fret) matches the open first string. Let the notes sustain while you are doing this. Then use the sequence in Example 1 to set the intonation for the remaining five strings. (Observe that the fingered notes in each diagram spell a major triad: root, 3rd, 5th, root.) The sequence for the third string is especially helpful for setting an unwrapped G string's intonation.

A word of advice: At the beginning of each sequence, be exacting when tuning the first fretted note to the open string. If the pitch of each pair of strings is not exactly the same, the rest of the sequence will be useless. The sequence beginning with the third string works equally well for the electric bass, even though the pitch is one octave lower.

Example 1.

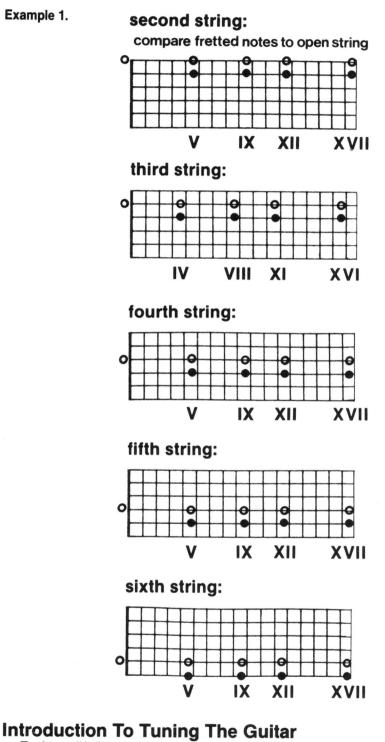

second string:

compare fretted notes to open string

V　　IX　XII　　XVII

third string:

IV　　VIII　XI　　XVI

fourth string:

V　　IX　XII　　XVII

fifth string:

V　　IX　XII　　XVII

sixth string:

V　　IX　XII　　XVII

Introduction To Tuning The Guitar

Tuning well is like playing well—it takes practice and time. One thing is certain: Both are equally important for good musicianship. A few out-of-tune strings can destroy the beauty of the best piano in the world. And one out-of-tune guitar can foul up the sound of an entire symphony orchestra.

Through the years, I have watched really fine players frequently reach up and tweak one key and then another while playing. The chances of their guitars being in tune at any one time are remote, to say the least. Their single-line melodies were not offensive, but

Tuning The Guitar

One of the most familiar methods of tuning the guitar is shown in Example 2.

Example 2.

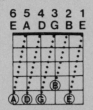

Assuming that the tension will not vary enough to affect the neck angle, we can proceed to fine-tune.

Step 1: Tune the high E string to the precise desired pitch.

Step 2: Tune the fretted E (5th fret, B string) to the open (first-string) E.

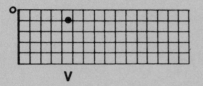

V

Now cross check by comparing the B harmonic (12th string, B string) to the fretted B at the 7th fret, first string. Remember to let the strings sustain, and listen carefully for a wave.

harm.

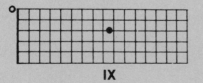

VII   XII

Step 3: Because of the characteristics of unwrapped third strings, this method is very helpful for nylon as well as metal strings. Tune the fretted E (9th fret, G string) to the open high E string.

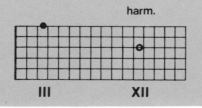

IX

Cross check by playing the harmonic at the 12th fret of the G string to the fretted G (3rd fret, high E string).

harm.

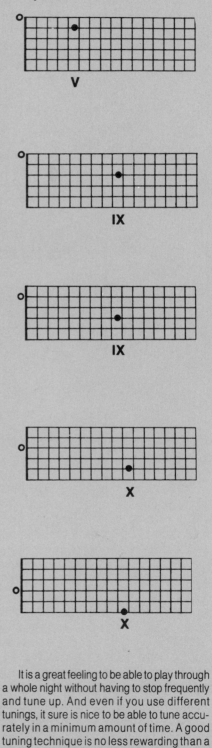

III   XII

Step 4: Tune the fretted B (9th fret, D string) to the open B string.

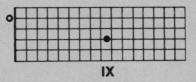

IX

Check the tuning by playing the harmonic at the 12th fret on the D string to the fretted D (3rd fret, B string).

harm.

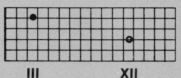

III   XII

Step 5: Tune the fretted G (10th fret, A string) to the open G.

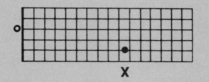

X

Compare the harmonic produced at the 12th fret on the A string with the fretted A (2nd fret, G string).

harm.

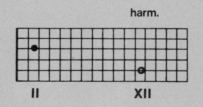

II   XII

Step 6: Tune the fretted D (10th fret, low E string) to the open D string.

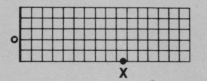

X

Cross check by referencing the harmonic at the 12th fret on the low E string with the fretted E (2nd fret, D string).

harm.

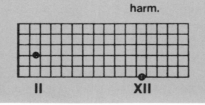

II   XII

The quick checking sequence in example 3 can be especially helpful to players like me who change to different tunings during the course of a performance. Just the tension change of one string can throw out the tuning of some of the others, so sometimes it is important to have a quick sequence to avoid going into the next song out of tune. The two strings can be picked simultaneously by using the pick in combination with your 3rd finger.

Example 3.

It is a great feeling to be able to play through a whole night without having to stop frequently and tune up. And even if you use different tunings, it sure is nice to be able to tune accurately in a minimum amount of time. A good tuning technique is no less rewarding than a good playing technique, and certainly no less important.

when it came time to sustain even a major chord, it was not acceptable.

Accepting the fact that humans vary from day to day, we need a tuning system that works on bad days as well as good ones, that works when we have to tune while instruments are playing in the background, or when we have hangovers, etc. Have you ever noticed that on some days everything you attempt to play turns out just perfect? The very next day, the opposite is true, and everything turns into zilch! Well, the same holds true with our attempts at tuning.

With some practice and application, the following method of tuning should work well—or at least get you into the ball park—even under the most adverse conditions. Although this sequence can be accomplished quickly, until you have developed the skill, be patient and take your time. Let the notes sustain, and listen carefully for differences in pitch between the two strings.

The single most difficult thing a teacher confronts is trying to instruct a beginning student to tune the guitar. Relating two tones is, at first, out of reach for the average beginner and a source of frustration for the dedicated teacher. But the ability to tune—like the ability to play the instrument—can be developed.

More and more players today depend entirely upon electronic tuners, and unfortunately, they are becoming the victims of self-inflicted "tin ears syndrome." I do not use a strobe tuner in setting intonation, as each instrument has its own inherent intonation characteristics, just as a fine concert grand piano. Don't get me wrong—I'm not an enemy of electronic tuners, but in a lot of cases the players are not trying to develop the skill of tuning the instrument to *itself*. The pleasure of listening to a well-tuned guitar is no less than the pleasure of listening to a well-tuned piano.

What does it take to develop the ability to tune and intonate the guitar well? Let's start with the number-one requisite: to be able to differentiate between two tones. Try this on yourself or your student: Tune the fretted *E* at the 5th fret on the second string to the same pitch as the open high *E* string. Pick the two strings simultaneously. If the pitch of both strings is identical, they will sound like one string with no vibrato or "wave" (see Figure 4).

Figure 4.

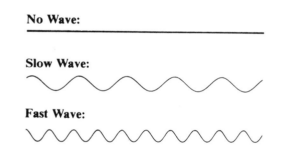

No Wave:

Slow Wave:

Fast Wave:

If there is a slight difference in pitch, there will be a slow vibrato or beating. As the pitch differential is increased, the vibrato's speed also increases. Listening for and being able to recognize the wave, or pulse, is the whole secret to fine-tuning the guitar. In order for the wave to be heard and recognized, the two strings must be allowed to sustain as long as possible, because if the pitch of the strings is very close—but not quite exact—it takes time for the wave to build in intensity. So when it comes to a well-tuned musical instrument, remember: Close only counts in horseshoes!

The differential wave is not confined to music alone. Those of us who fly light twin-engine airplanes use the wave to synchronize the RPM of the two propellers. If you want to make your passengers uncomfortable, fly with the props out of sync. By the same token, if you want to make an audience uncomfortable, play with out-of-tune instruments. Hopefully, this illustrates that you do not have to be a "gifted musician" to be able to recognize the difference between two tones.

Now that we have dispelled the mysteries of tuning the guitar, let's try a tuning sequence that works on good *and* bad days. First, let's consider that the guitar's neck is stressed for a certain tension of the strings. If this tension is changed, the angle of the neck changes accordingly. For example, if you have to tune to a higher pitch (increased tension), the neck will bend forward. If you started tuning from the high *E*, by the time you tuned across the strings to the low *E*, the higher strings would be flat because of the forward bending of the neck. The opposite is true if you have to tune to a lower pitch. It is therefore most important to tune (by whatever method) to the *approximate* desired pitch before you attempt to "fine tune" the instrument.

By Johnny Smith

The Necessity Of Reading Music

Guitar Player, June 1979.

Guitar players (regardless of style) have the reputation of not being able to read music, or at least the reputation for being poor readers. This attitude has changed slightly in the past decade, but not enough to convince many musicians that the guitarist should be allowed to sit in with a symphony orchestra. Although this article will not involve any musical examples, it will suggest some very practical ways in which to improve your reading skills.

First, I think we should list several guitar styles and show the levels of reading ability among guitarists in each genre. This analysis is based on my 20 years of experience in crossing all types of guitar players, and by no means is the final word (there are plenty of exceptions); however, trust me that the general assumptions are accurate. The list starts with the best guitar readers and ends with the worst and takes into account the overall ability to read music, knowledge of the fingerboard, sight-reading facility, horizontal reading (single notes), and vertical reading (notes stacked upon one another—chords, counterpoint, etc).

1. Studio	4. Rock	7. Blues
2. Jazz	5. Pop	8. Flamenco
3. Classical	6. Country	9. Folk

It's not hard to guess that studio guitarists would be the best readers. They have usually spent the most time practicing their reading in preparation for becoming session players. In general, jazz guitarists have also spent a great deal of time with written music, and in many cases have attended universities that stress the reading of music. Classical guitarists usually spend a large amount of time in learning to read music; their goal is usually to learn how to read well enough in order to read or transcribe classical guitar compositions and then memorize them. Unfortunately, classical guitarists are usually poor sight-readers.

Starting with the rock, pop, and country guitarists, the levels of reading drop considerably for a few simple reasons. In the case of the rock guitarist, he or she usually starts to pick up the guitar by ear. This is by no means a detriment; in fact, I've noticed that many rock and pop guitarists have better ear training than the studio, jazz, or classical players. As we know, some of the most innovative guitar playing has come from rock guitarists who did not read a note (e.g., Jimi Hendrix). So if you plan to be in that category you need not read further. However, for those of you who are a little more practical, you can see that the days of the rock guitarist not needing to read music are over. There are just too many guitarists out there competing for the same job.

The blues, flamenco, and folk guitarists are usually the worst readers, but I don't mean any insult. The traditions for learning such styles run very deep, and in the past have had very little to do with reading written music.

Looking at this list of guitar stylists and their general reading abilities, you might get some idea of where you fit in. For example, if you are a folk guitarist looking to break into the studios, you just may have a great deal of work to do in the reading department.

There are several steps you can take right away to help improve your reading. First of all, give yourself this test to determine your weakest points:

1. Randomly select a note, such as Bb. Play it on each string, starting with the sixth up to the first, as fast as you can. For example, if you were using the note Bb, you would go from the sixth string's 6th fret to the fifth string's 1st fret, the fourth string's 8th fret, the third string's 3rd fret, the second string's 11th fret, and the first string's 6th fret. If you can complete the test from the sixth string to the first string in between one and two second's time, you have an excellent knowledge of the fingerboard. Three to four seconds is average; if it takes longer than that—well, you know you need some work. Try this exercise with all the chromatic tones.

2. Write down on music paper as many random notes as you can think of. Use natural notes, sharps, flats, and notes way above and below the staff. Make sure you assign *no* rhythmic value to the notes. Read these notes on the guitar as fast as you can. Then put down the guitar and merely recite them, including all flats, naturals, and sharps (for example, *A, F♯, B♮, D,* etc). If you were able to recite the notes quickly, then your basic knowledge of the staff, ledger lines, etc. is probably adequate. If you slowed down when you played the same notes on the instrument, your knowledge of the fingerboard is possibly weak. If you did well *playing* the notes on your guitar but slowed down considerably when you recited them, then your basic understanding of the notes on the staff is probably weak. By the way, this test should include both treble and bass clefs; I believe it helps *greatly* for a guitarist to be able to read in both clefs.

3. This part of the test involves writing out a rhythmic pattern with no pitch content. Copy the rhythmic values from a piece of music, or make up your own. Next, either sing or tap out the rhythm and see how your performance compares to parts 1 and 2 of the test. If you have an easy time with them, but you're having trouble tapping out the correct rhythm of part 3, then you'll know the weakest part of your reading ability and you can concentrate on improving it.

Be honest with yourself, and if you really can't accurately pinpoint what part you're weak in, try the tests with a friend or a teacher. If you're weak in all three areas, really get to work!

Currently in the United States (and probably abroad) there are more guitarists earning a living professionally than ever before. The competitiveness is incredible, and if you don't know how to read music your chances of making it will become less and less real. The 1960s witnessed an incredible boom in rock music and many people took up the guitar. The children of the '60s are coming out in droves and a whole lot of them are monster guitar players!

If I could give any advice to young guitar players, it would be simply two things: Learn to read music, and study ear training. If you can hear a piece of music and play it immediately, and also read music well, then you're going to cut down your competition immensely and have a good chance of making it in the music business.

Here's a list of some books that may help you practice your reading:

Method For Clarinet, by H. Close (from Carl Fischer, 62 Cooper Square. New York, NY 10003). This book is only for single-note reading, but since the clarinet and guitar have basically the same range it is an excellent study.

Develop Sight Reading, Vols. 1 and 2, by Gaston Dufresne (from Chas. Colin Music. 315 W. 53rd St., New York, NY 10019). This is also for single-note reading, but if you can get through the complete book you've got it made.

Rhythms Complete, Vols. 1, 2, 3, and 4. by Bugs Bower (from Chas. Colin).

Progressive Steps To Syncopation For The Modern Drummer, by Ted Reed (from Ted Reed, Box 327, Clearwater, FL 33515). This book is great for part 3 of the test that we just covered.

Basic Jazz Conception For Saxophone, Vols. 1 and 2, by Lennie Niehaus (from Try Publishing, 845 Vine, Hollywood, CA 90038).

Advanced Duets, Vols. 1, 2, and 3, by Bob Nelson (from Chas. Colin).

John McLaughlin And The Mahavishnu Orchestra (from Warner Bros. Publ., 9200 Sunset Blvd., Suite 530, Los Angeles, CA 90069).

The Howard Roberts Guitar Book, by Howard Roberts and Jimmy Stewart (from Playback, Box 4278. North Hollywood, CA 91607).

Joe Pass Guitar Style (from Warner Bros.).

Finger-Picking Styles For Guitar, by Happy Traum (from Oak Publ., 33 W. 60th St., New York, NY 10023).

Six Black Blues Guitarists, by Woody Mann (from Oak Publ.).

Electric Bass lines, by Carol Kaye (from Warner Bros.). This book is great for bass clef reading.

The Art Of The Folk Blues Guitar, by Jerry Silverman (from Oak Publ.).

Carcassi Method For The Guitar, by G.C. Santisteban (from Oliver Ditson Co., dist. by Theodore Presser, Lancaster and Presser Pl., Bryn Mawr, PA 19010).

Andres Segovia—Studies For The Guitar By Fernando Sor (from Edward B. Marks Corp, dist. by Belwin-Mills, Melville, NY 11746).

The Lee Ritenour Book, by Lee Ritenour (from Flat Five Publ., dist. by Professional Music Products, 1114 N. Gilbert St., Anaheim, Ca 92801).

Eric Clapton Deluxe (from Warner Bros.).

Jean-Luc Ponty (from Warner Bros.).

The Jazz Styles Of Maynard Ferguson (from Warner Bros.).

This list goes to show you that reading everything and anything available will help you. Go to it, and believe me it will pay big dividends.

Lee Ritenour

Notation: Chord Symbols And Road Signs

Guitar Player, **February 1986.**

One of the most basic musical skills you should develop is reading and understanding charts. We'll start with chord symbols. This is an area that gets convoluted and confusing because different geographical regions develop different symbolic codes, and different transcribers and copyists develop their own styles and idiosyncracies. An all-purpose rhythm-section chart can be slightly wacky, as a pianist or bassist may be used to symbols and/or voicings that may leave a guitarist clueless.

Nevertheless, using good, old, no-sharps-or-flats C as the example, here is a list of *some* of the varying chord symbols I have encountered (see chart below).

Symbol	Chord	Notes
C	C major	C,E,G
Cm, Cmin, Cmi, C7	C minor	C, Eb, G
C7, Cdom7	C dominant 7th	C, E, G, Bb
Cmaj7, Cm7, C△7	C major 7th	C, E, G, B
Cm6, Cmi6, C-6	C minor 6th	C, Eb, G, A
Cm7, Cmi7, C-7	C minor 7th	C, Eb, G, Bb
Cm9, Cmi9, C-9	C minor 9th	C, Eb, G, Bb, D
C6, Cadd6	C 6th	C, E, G, A
C9	C 9th	C, E, G, Bb, D
C11	C 11th	C, E, G, Bb, D, F
C13	C 13th	C, E, G, Bb, D, F, A
C6/9	C add 6th add 9th	C, E, G, A, D
C/G	C major over a G bass note	G, C, E, G
C/E	C chord over an E bass note	E, C, E, G
Cmin (maj7)	C minor, add the major-scale 7th degree	C, Eb, G, B
C°, Cdim	C diminished	C, Eb, Gb
CØ, Cm7b5	C half-diminished, or C minor 7th lowered 5th	C, Eb, Gb, Bb
Cdim7, C°7	C diminished 7th	C, Eb, Gb, A
C7b9, C7-9, C7dim9	C7 lowered 9th	C, E, G, Bb, Db
C7#9, C7+9, C7aug9	C7 raised 9th	C, E, G, Bb, D#
C+, Caug	C augmented	C, E, G#
Csus4, Csus	C suspended 4th	C, G, F
C5, C (no 3rd)	C 5th, C power 5th C no 3rd	C, G
Cadd2, Cadd9	C add 2nd, or C add 9th	C, E, G, D

Extended chords, such as *C11, C13, Cm11,* and *Cm13,* theoretically contain every building-block partial note. For example, *Cm11* contains *C, Eb, G, Bb, D,* and *F*; *Cm13* contains *C, Eb, G, Bb, D, F,* and *A.*

Of course, guitarists cannot practically play seven-note chords—even most six-note chords can be next to impossible. So in the interest of practicality, the first note to eliminate is usually the perfect 5th. Then you start to lose the compound (outside the octave) partials that are not figured into the chord symbol, until you've got something that is manageable. In other words, even though a *C13* is technically supposed to have the notes, *C, E, G, Bb, D, F,* and *A,* the two most common guitar voicings are Examples 4 and 5, which have only the notes *C, Bb, E,* and *A* (really just a *C7add13*) and *C, E, Bb, D,* and *A* (*C9add13*), respectively.

I've also provided fingerings of some of the chords listed here in Example 6. Keep in mind that there are many ways to "voice" a chord, and therefore lots of other available ways to form it on the fingerboard. You should also notice *notes* in the chart indicate chord spellings only. In practice, certain notes are commonly omitted and rearranged. You could test yourself by playing the chords in Example 6, separating and identifying each note in the chord, and then figuring out how each note *functions* to make the chord what it is.

Example 4.

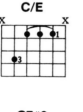

C13

Example 5.

C13

Example 6.

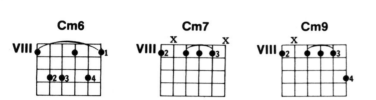

Cm6   Cm7   Cm9

C9   C/G   C/E   Cm(maj7)

Cdim7   Cm7♭5   C7#9   C7♭9

Cadd9

Cadd9   Cadd9

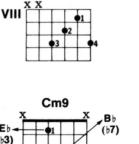

Cm9

Usually a bracketed bit of extra information means this is something unusual to add on to the chord symbol immediately preceding; *e.g., Cm(maj7).* (A slash is also commonly used.) Symbols such as *C∅* and *Cm7♭5* denote the same chord. If you see "add2" or "add9," you simply *add* the 2nd or 9th to the *full* chord symbol preceding (including the *3rd*); if you see "sus4," however, *eliminate* the 3rd from the chord.

When a whole chord symbol is bracketed on a chart, such as (*G♭m9*), it usually means that it is optional, but a nice suggestion to employ if you are up to it. When you see N.C., it stands for "no chord," so you lay out, pick out the single-note melody line, or follow the bass part.

By Rik Emmett

Tips For Beginners From Eddie Van Halen

Guitar Player, **July 1984.**

Rock and roll is feeling. And after you know most of the basics—chords, rhythms, scales, and bends, which I'll begin discussing in a minute—getting that feeling is just about the most important aspect of playing guitar.

In my opinion, you can't learn to play rock and roll by taking lessons. Although a teacher can show you certain things, such as songs and licks, you still have to sit down and learn how things feel by listening. My biggest influence was Eric Clapton when he was with Cream and John Mayall's Bluesbreakers. I learned his solos to "Crossroads" [from Cream's *Wheels Of Fire*, RSO, 3802] and "Sitting On Top Of The World" [Cream, *Goodbye*, RSO, 3013] note-for-note by slowing them down to 16 RPM on my dad's turntable. By taking licks off records and listening, I developed a feel for rock and roll. If you want to play, that's the same kind of thing you'll have to do. Eventually, you'll take the phrases and rhythm patterns you've copped and begin to put your own mark on them.

One of the areas that guys put too much emphasis on is equipment. Once when Van Halen was on tour, we were opening for Ted Nugent and he was standing there watching me play, wondering how I did it. The next day at the soundcheck when I wasn't there, he asked our roadie if he could plug into my stuff. Of course, it still sounded like Ted. In other words, it doesn't really matter what you're playing through. Too many guys think a certain player's sound has to do with equipment, but it doesn't make any difference. Your sound is in your fingers and brain.

If you're going to learn to play lead, get an electric guitar. It doesn't have to be an expensive one (I started on a cheapie Teisco Del Rey). Acoustic guitars aren't good for learning lead, because you can't play up very high on the neck and they take heavier-gauge strings, which makes it hard to bend notes. (I use light ones, Fender XLs.) Also, you don't really need an amp at first, unless you're in a band. When I'm noodling around the house, I rarely plug in.

Most beginners want to learn lead because they think it's cool. Consequently, they never really develop good rhythm skills. Since most of a rock guitarist's time is spent playing rhythm, it's important to learn to do it well. Learning lead should come after you can play solid backup and have the sound of the chords in your head.

Playing blues progressions is the best place to start learning, because they're so basic, and they form the foundation for a lot of rock tunes. After you've got one or two patterns down in a couple of keys, you can start noodling with lead guitar. Examples 7 and 8 are two shuffle patterns in the keys of *A* and *E*, respectively. Memorize them as soon as possible. Eventually, you'll want to learn them in some of the other common rock keys, such as *C, D,* and *G.* "Ice Cream Man," from our first album, and "Blues Breaker," which I did on Brian May's *Star Fleet Project,* are 12-bar blues. [*Ed. Note: In the tablature, the horizontal lines represent the guitar's strings (the uppermost line is the first string), while the numbers denote frets.*]

Example 7.

Example 7 (continued).

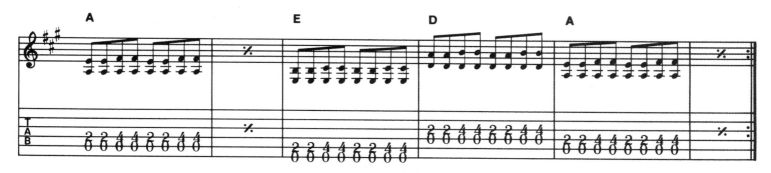

Example 8.

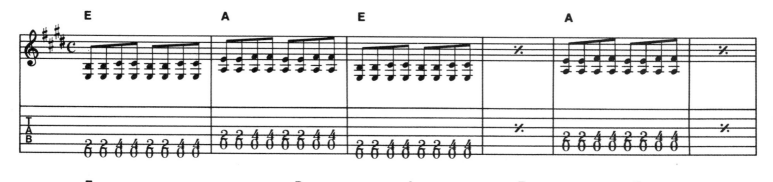

I learned my first chords from a beginning guitar book that showed the usual *C, D, Db,* and *Em* down at the nut. But I rarely play chords like that. Listen to the difference between a regular *C* chord and this one in Example 9, which sounds much more rock and roll.

Example 9.

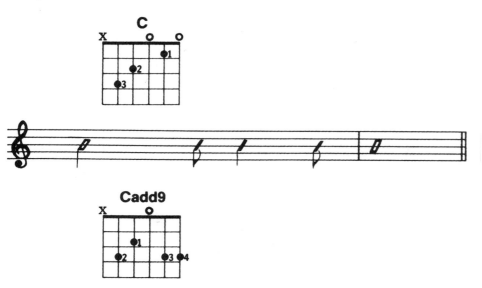

For a *G* chord I use this fingering in Example 10 (slightly muffle the bass notes with the heel of your right hand).

Example 10.

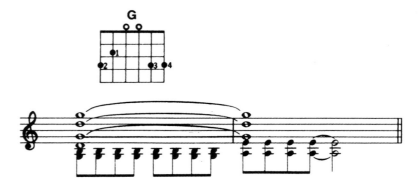

A lot of rock players mainly use barre chords, which employ the left-hand 1st finger to cover all six strings at a particular fret, but I usually just two-note it, like the beginning of "On Fire" from our LP *Van Halen* (Example 11).

Example 11.

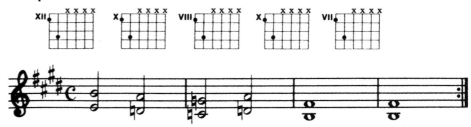

Rhythm patterns can often be made more interesting by incorporating different riffs. Example 12 illustrates this. It's similar to what I do in "Ain't Talkin' 'Bout Love," also from *Van Halen*. It features a simple bass hook; try using all downstrokes for the two-note parts (more on right-hand picking in a moment).

Example 12.

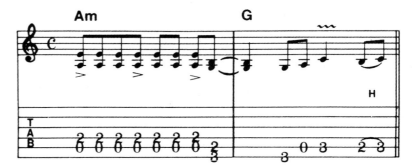

Later in "Ain't Talkin' 'Bout Love," I play the same chords in an arpeggio style. This is another good way to keep things from getting boring (Example 13).

Example 13.

Before we start working on playing lead, I want to talk about right-hand picking. Guys have pointed out that I hold my pick in two ways: with my thumb and middle finger (see Figure 5), and with my thumb, index, and middle (see Figure 6). Remember that most players don't pick the way I do, so what works for me might not work for you. The important thing about using the pick is that you *alternate* the picking direction: down, up, down, up, etc., as shown in Example 14. This method really increases the efficiency of your picking hand. Once you get used to alternating strokes, you'll be able to pick without having to think about it.

Example 14.

Figure 5.

Figure 6.

The position for the blues scale (shown in Example 15) is the one most often used by blues and rock players. This scale fits many chords, including the *entire* 12-bar progression, and since it has five notes, it's called the pentatonic scale (penta is Latin for "five"). If you already know this position, but still can't play lead very well, then you haven't worked with it enough. Once you learn some hammer-ons, pull-offs, slides, and bends, and how they're incorporated into licks, you'll see why the position is so common (be sure to use alternate picking).

The next two patterns in Example 16 are the same as the one we just looked at, only in different locations. Knowing several patterns enables you to play over the entire length of the fingerboard. Also, different positions lend themselves to different licks.

Another common scale position is the long form shown in Examples 17 and 18, which spans from the 3rd to the 12th fret. Note that when it descends (Example 18), the notes are played on different strings; however, you can go backwards through the ascending pattern (if you do, use your 1st finger to shift downward). Notice that when you go up, the 3rd finger is used to get to each new position. Also, the area around the 7th fret can produce some especially nice phrases.

Example 15.

Example 16.

Example 17.

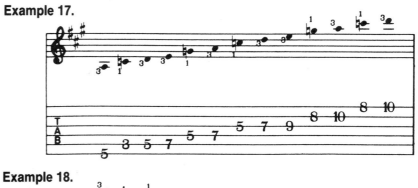

Example 18.

Once you have these scale patterns memorized, it's time to learn how to move them to other keys. For instance, the first pattern becomes an *E* scale when moved to the 12th fret. You can easily figure this out by moving the root of the scale up the fingerboard chromatically (the root is the note that has the same name as the scale). For example, on the sixth string the note at the 5th fret is an *A*; at the 6th fret it's an *A♯* (or a *B♭*—they're the same); at the 7th fret it's a *B*, and so on until you get to the 12th fret. Figure 7 shows the complete chromatic scale so you can move other patterns on your own (once you get to the end of the scale, *G♯*, continue ascending by starting over at *A*). As long as you know the name of the scale or chord you're starting with, you can move up or down through the chromatic scale; each letter represents one fret (beware of open strings).

Figure 7.

| A | A♯(B♭) | B | C | C♯(D♭) | D | D♯(E♭) | E | F | F♯(G♭) | G | G♯(A♭) |

But knowing note locations is just the beginning. The next step is to start learning the building blocks of licks: hammer-ons, pull-offs, bends, and slides. Hammer-ons and pull-offs can give the notes you play fluidity and speed. The phrases in Example 19 are a few short examples for the scale position at the 5th fret. From here it's your responsibility to transfer the techniques to other phrases and positions.

Example 19.

Bending is probably the technique most often associated with blues and rock soloing, and for that reason it's the most important one to learn. If you're a beginner, there are a couple of things to watch out for. First, don't overshoot the bend. By that I mean don't bend a note beyond where you intend to go. And once a note is bent, be careful not to use too much finger vibrato—a singing effect produced by rapidly wiggling a string with a finger of your left hand right after it's been played. If your vibrato wavers too much, you'll overshoot the bend and it'll sound weird.

Here's an exercise for developing bending accuracy (Example 20). If you can bend with the left-hand 4th finger, fine; but most players use the 3rd finger because it's stronger. The other fingers can support the one doing the bending. Most bends in rock and blues go up one whole-step; get the correct note in your head by playing the *A* on the second string, 10th fret. Practice bending right up to the *A*. If you hold the note for a while, use slight vibrato.

Now let's learn the bend in combination with some other notes (see Example 21). (A reverse bend *starts* with a bent note, and then releases it.)

Example 20.

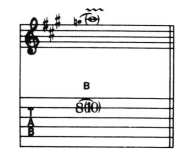

Example 21.

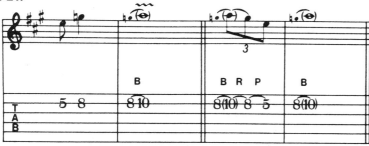

Lots of guys ask which notes I like to bend the most, and I always say *all* of them. And that's true, depending on the song I'm playing. However, some notes are bent more than others. The example we just looked at uses one of the most commonly bent notes. Remember its position in relation to the scale pattern at the 5th fret—it's on the second string and played with the 3rd finger—so you can use it in other keys. Two other good notes to bend, also played with the 3rd finger, are located on the third string, 7th fret (*D*; see Figure 8) and first string, 8th fret, (*C*). Here are some licks using both notes,

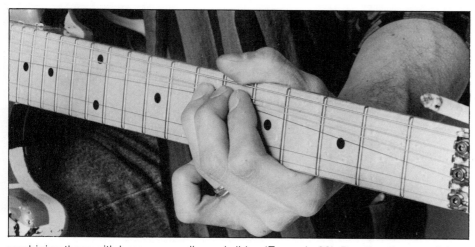

Figure 8.

combining them with hammers, pulls, and slides (Example 22). Practice them until they become second nature; then find their location in the other scale patterns. Once things feel comfortable, work on playing lead in different keys and with a variety of rhythms.

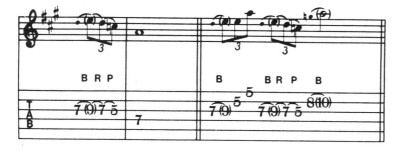

Example 22.

Example 22 (continued).

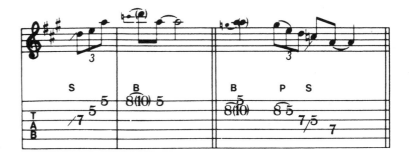

Sometimes I think of a new technique or lick at the strangest times. When I got the idea for right-hand tapping, I was in the bathroom with my guitar. This technique is often written incorrectly in books and played wrong, so here's how it works. To understand the idea (behind right-hand tapping), first play this trill with your left hand (see Example 23).

Now tap a finger of your right hand—I usually use the first or second—to produce the first note, and then pull it off of the string to sound the second (see Example 24 and Figure 9). The pull-off motion should be toward you, and should slightly catch the string. Whole descending scales can be played in this way; go back and try it with the first blues pattern we discussed.

Example 23.

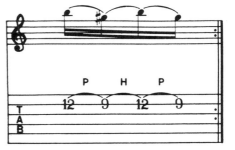

Figure 9.

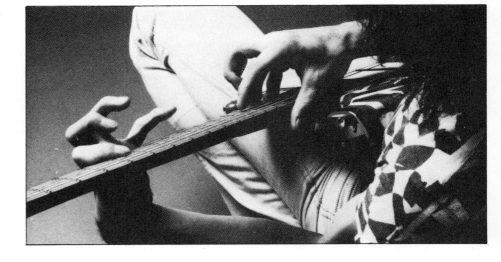

Example 24.

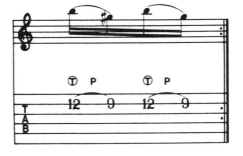

Once you understand the basic moves of tapping (sounding the note with your right hand and pulling off), then you're ready to apply it to a lick. Example 25 shows a thing I do in the last part of "Eruption," from *Van Halen* (it can also be played on the third string). It's really easy, and makes a great exercise. Notice that after you tap and pull off, you then hammer down to get the third note. Experiment enough with this technique and you'll realize you can get many other combinations.

Example 25.

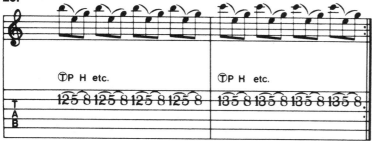

Another easy right-hand technique is harmonic tapping. Examples of this can be heard on "Spanish Fly," "Women In Love" [both from *Van Halen II*], "Eruption," and "Top Jimmy" [*1984*]. In order to produce a harmonic, just tap 12 frets above a note, directly on the fret, as shown in Example 26 (remove your right-hand finger quickly). Although you can do this technique on an acoustic instrument, you'll get better results on an electric (see Figure 10).

Example 26.

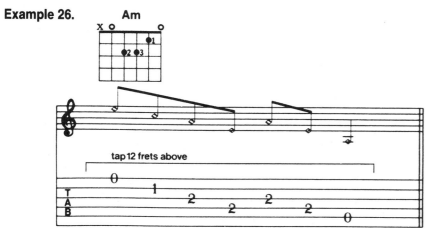

Figure 10.

Now that you know some of the basic ingredients of rock and roll, remember that your playing has to have feeling and taste. The goal is to make music, not always to play machine gun-type stuff. To me, music is entertainment. You shouldn't be playing it to save the world or show people how great you are. It's just supposed to make you happy, make you cry, make you get horny, or whatever. If it doesn't do that, then it's not music. And remember: You learn by making mistakes. Don't be afraid to try something new. If I'm thrown into an unfamiliar situation, such as playing with Allan Holdsworth, I don't panic. Sometimes I skin my knees, but most of the time I land on my feet. My dad has a Dutch saying that puts it much better than I can: Translated, it means, "Ride your bicycle straight through." If you screw up, just keep going.

As told to Jim Ferguson

Chapter 2:
Rhythm

Playing Rhythm

Guitar Player, February 1979.

It seems that almost all the players who are striving to be professionals are geared to learning how to play *lead* and *rhythm* guitar. However, most guitarists—especially young ones—usually concentrate on lead playing: improvising, melodies, sound, etc. The rhythm playing is almost always an afterthought (in my case, it was no different). However, from the Beatles on, the rhythm guitar has always been the most important guitar on rock and pop recordings. The solo lead guitar is usually the "spice" that goes on last to fill in the record or to provide a short solo; the rhythm part holds it all together.

Now, if you happen to be a great soloist with a style of your own, you probably won't have much trouble carving out a career playing the guitar. I have seen a couple of great players bite the dust in the studio because they would not resign themselves to playing a rhythm guitar part, though. In most cases, not every musician out there is *always* going to get to play his or her own music. At some point in most careers the player has to accompany other performers. I realized this while fairly young and made a study of all the different styles of rhythm playing. In comparison to the 1930s and 1940s, when all you had to deal with was Freddie Green's style of comping in pianist Count Basie's band, things have really changed!

Currently, there are too many styles of guitar accompaniment to include here, but they are worth mentioning. Simply, you could begin with the most basic accompaniment known to the guitar—folk music. This category would include a wide variety of styles stretching to the most contemporary folk accompaniment (e.g., Joni Mitchell, James Taylor, etc.). On the other side would be included basic rock and roll accompaniment—the heavy metal groups, power trios, punk rockers, and others from the '60s and '70s. These would include the Rolling Stones, Cream, and Jimi Hendrix up to Van Halen and so forth. Besides those two huge categories, you would have to include country music, rhythm and blues (R&B), disco, Latin, middle of the road (MOR), and any varieties of jazz and progressive rock. Do you still think a good rhythm guitar player has it easy?

The most important point about rhythm playing is that it can be extremely creative, and to come up with the "perfect part" for a song with a band or on a record is no easy feat. There is also another facet to being the rhythm guitar player: Specifically referring to the recording medium, one has to be careful of how much "space" one takes up on a record. There might be one, two, or three other guitar players on the same session. Your part not only has to work with the song and the vocal line (if there is one), but you also have to interact with the drummer, bass player, keyboardist, and especially the other guitar players.

Let's take an example of some possible rhythm guitar parts. Suppose we stretch the point a little and assume that there are ten guitar players on a recording session (believe me, there are people in Hollywood who have tried that). And let's also assume that there are only two chords in the song (not so farfetched). The "groove" is a sort of funk-R&B tune with the bass player and drummer playing off of the rhythm shown in Example 1.

Example 1.

The first and second guitar parts are definitely the easiest and the most boring. However, sometimes such parts are the most essential. If the guitar players on this session were ranked according to seniority, then the newer and younger ones would play these parts. As shown in Example 2, the first pattern is only whole-notes. The producer would probably prefer it in open-string chord voicing, if possible, and very full sounding (using five- or six-string chords). You might be asked to play it with a phaser or on a 12-string guitar. The second guitar would be called on to play "a tight backbeat," preferably with a Fender Stratocaster or Telecaster. Guitar number three is an extremely

Example 2.

important part; it is a copy of what the bass player and drummer have started. This part is locked in with them.

Guitar number four has started the first melody-rhythm part. It still contributes to the rhythm function, and at the same time includes a little countermelody part. In Los Angeles we refer to this style as "skank," patterned after the style of Ray Parker of Raydio, a great rhythm player (to give credit where credit is due, I believe Jay Graydon, another fine studio guitarist, coined the phrase). In order to play this part you must mute all six strings with your left hand, except when you're playing the melody notes. Strum all six strings, and let the pick and your first finger make contact with the strings.

Guitar number five has a little more percussive sound with its muted notes and "shotgun" effect. Guitar number six has come up with an "answer" part to guitars four and five; this melody-rhythm part comes in the second bar instead of the first. Guitar number seven is mostly a fill part, and intervals of thirds and fourths are very popular here.

Guitar number eight is very valuable. It can add some extra energy to the whole rhythm section by droning on one note. Guitar number nine is adding more of a pretty part by fingerpicking through the chords; this part could be played on either electric or acoustic. Guitar number ten doesn't know what to do. Everything is filled up, so he or she pulls out a wah-wah and "scratches" a reggae pattern with no chords.

In the final result, there are just two chords, but every player has to come up with a different part that fits. In most cases the arranger does not write down these kinds of rhythm patterns, so it's up to the players. If you were the tenth guitar player, could you have found a part?

By Lee Ritenour

22 Rhythm Patterns For All Occasions

Guitar Player, August 1977.

Rock guitarists are very valued specialists on typical club dates because they are usually able to do what the other players cannot: present authentic rock music. From the days when Elvis first made the guitar synonymous with rock music, the guitarist was an integral part of any rock group. But it was not until around 1964 when the Beatles turned the form into a cultural phenomenon that the so-called society bands realized that rock music would have to be in their repertoire or they'd be out of work.

Initially, this realization came about when guests at parties began requesting rock tunes. The typical country club/hotel band, however, was unable to respond to the demand. When the seriousness of rock finally became apparent, the bands began to learn a few tunes they thought sounded like rock. But the likes of piano trios or groups with old-time horn sections, all raised on standard music and usually abhorring the new sound, could hardly be expected to satisfy the tastes of the growing number of sophisticated rock aficionados. Enter the rock guitarist.

Now that the presence of the rock guitarist had become essential on the club date, be it for a single engagement, with a small group or with a big band, there arose a considerable demand for guitarists who could handle the special requirements of club date work. Bands for such occasions are often made up of musicians brought together for a limited engagement, prior to which they were probably unknown to each other. All in such "pickup" groups may be capable of playing well, but the ad hoc nature of their meeting begins to define the rather unique role of the rock guitarist.

Most rock bands, after all, rehearse. If they play Top 40 tunes, they try to copy every note of the record. If they perform original music, the arrangements are meticulously prepared by the band so that every musician has a part, with a structured division of responsibilities so that it's possible to observe that there is a lead guitar and a rhythm guitar, to say nothing of the important contributions of the bass, organ, and drums.

The club date situation, however, is quite different. Often, the band has never rehearsed. Even if they had, it would not have been with the rock guitarist. Accordingly, the club date orchestra is likely to have very little idea of what the guitarist is going to do. Moreover, the chances are good that the orchestra members don't like rock music and are not very skilled in that area. All this is to say that the rock guitarist on a club date is required to "carry" the band when rock is to be played. Indeed, the rock player must learn his songs based upon the assumption that the support he will receive from the rest of the band will be nonexistent to minimal. While this is perhaps overstating the case somewhat, the assumption will permit the guitarist to sound great regardless of the quality and inclination of his sidemen.

Based upon the foregoing concept, the club date rock guitar player must back his singing with strong, biting, rhythmic, slashing, full chords, all the while placing solid emphasis upon the bass notes in the chords. In addition, the rock guitarist must: have the proper equipment, set amp controls to complement his style; structure songs to avoid empty solos; avoid rhythms too complex or obscure to dance to without superior rehearsed drumming; develop a commercial repertoire designed to appeal to the broadest possible audience.

Of these various "do's," all of which are important, the most critical is the combination of playing forceful rhythms with full chords, because rhythms are the very basis of the rock guitarist's unique role in the club date field.

The guitar occupies the singular position of being both a melodic and rhythmic instrument at the same time. Since on a club date, there is no rhythm guitarist or lead guitarist as such and, as noted, rarely a set rehearsed group, the guitarist must handle both areas at once while setting the pace and carrying the band. All this will emerge from the rhythms *he* establishes.

The Vital Club Date Rhythm Patterns.

There are two ways to lay down strong rhythm patterns. One is to strum chords alone. The other is to combine single notes with portions of chords. Both methods can be effective but the latter should predominate in club-date work because it has more character, therefore compensating for the lack of support from the other players.

With the exception of a small group of super club-date rock players, the primary error made by rock guitarists is that they idly strum chords. Although they may have good timing, an obvious prerequisite in any event, their strumming lacks drive, push, force, strength, and *character*. The good club-date guitarist, on the other hand, establishes a meaningful rhythm that has a feel and pattern that dancers can groove on and which the band can readily follow.

Here are 22 dynamic, proven rhythm patterns which conform to the dictates of club date work.

Example 3 is probably the most basic rhythm in rock. It is very steady, danceable and easy to follow. Moreover, it's adaptable to both hard rock and softer interlude music, when a guitarist plays solo.

Example 4 is a variation of Example 3 which can be used to add interest, as taste dictates.

Example 5 adds the IV chord to the basic pattern to give rise to this variation of Example 3.

Example 3.

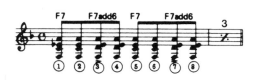
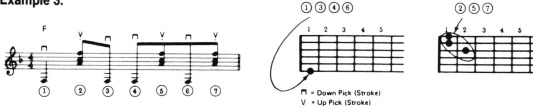

Example 4.

Example 5.

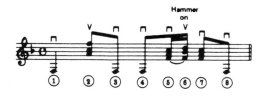
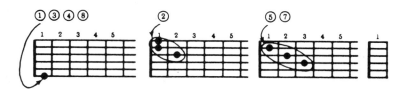

Example 6.

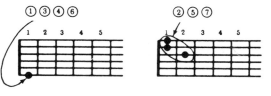

Example 7.

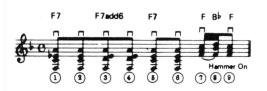
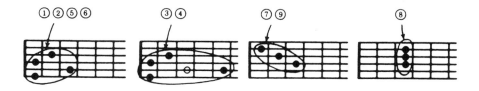
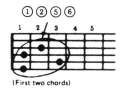

Example 6 is a rhythm that *must* be in every club date repertoire. It's a real smasher which typifies the hard driving rock of Chuck Berry, Jerry Lee Lewis, or Elvis Presley.

Example 7 adds a hint of the IV chord to the pattern in Example 6 to give us this effective variation.

Example 8 is another interesting variation of Example 6.

Example 9 offers still another way to interpret Example 6.

Example 10, although approaching a country and western sound, is most assuredly good solid rock, and it takes full advantage of the use of bass notes with the chords.

Example 11 is a slightly livelier variation of Example 10.

Example 12 is another variation of Example 10.

Example 13 is good to substitute in parts where Example 10 is appropriate, but where the tempo is too fast to comfortably fit in all the bass notes.

Example 8.

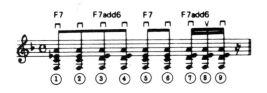

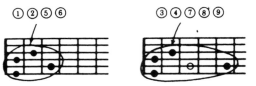

Example 9.

Example 10

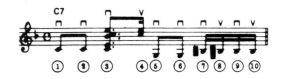

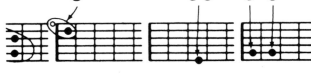

Example 11.

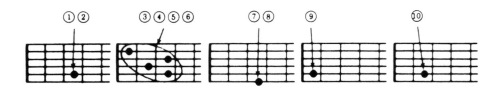

Example 12.

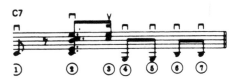

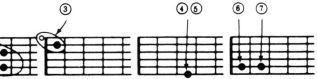

Example 13.

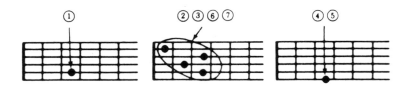

Example 14 is used in typical I-IV-V progression songs, along the lines of the Richie Valens' classic "La Bamba" and a number of Neil Diamond's earlier efforts, to cite just a few of many possible examples.

Example 15 is a prime example of the very necessary shuffle rhythm which is applicable to moderate tempos, for songs such as "Leroy Brown," "Does Anybody Really Know What Time It Is," "Do You Believe In Magic," etc., as well as to faster pace tunes such as "Rock Around The Clock" or "Rockin' Robin."

Example 16 is particularly appropriate for "broader" shuffle patterns, specifically "You're Sixteen."

Examples 17-23 are patterns found in the area of rhythms which might be defined as "funky."

Example 24 is an elementary version of the rhythm pattern necessary for the Hustle, the dance craze of 1975 (from Van McCoy hit of the same name).

Example 14.

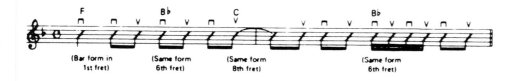

Example 15.

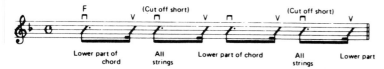

Example 16.

Example 17.

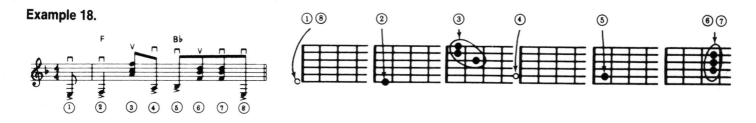

Example 18.

Example 19.

Example 20.

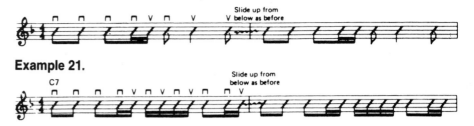

Example 21.

Example 22.

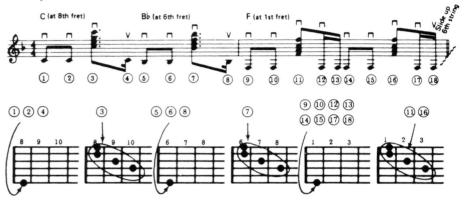

Example 23.

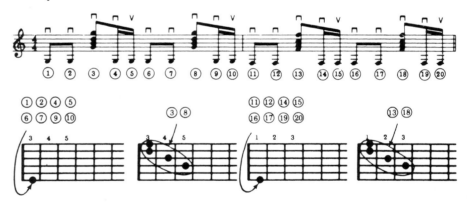

Example 24.

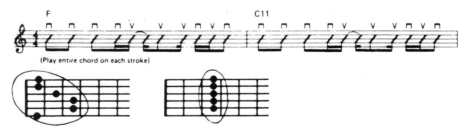

(Play entire chord on each stroke)

The choice of rhythm pattern appropriate for a particular song is within the artistic province of the individual guitarist. The problem in choosing the best rhythm is that the pattern of the record may be difficult to identify. A recording represents a finished product which has been mixed down from multiple tracks in a studio. There may in fact be more than one rhythm on the record derived from the drums, conga drums, lead guitar, rhythm guitar, horns, etc. Therefore, it is often difficult to determine which of the many patterns on the record is in the true feel of the song. Furthermore, this problem is compounded when learning a tune from the sheet music, if at that time only a memory of the recording remains. The solution, quite simply, is to experiment with the various rhythms and select the pattern which appears most comfortable.

By Bruce Bergman

Introduction To Some Different Chord Forms

All you rock and rollers probably know the stuff in the tabulature in Examples 25, 26 and 27. And if you play Example 25 four times, Example 26 two times, Example 25 another two times, then 27 once, 26 once, and 25 once, then a *B* or *B7* chord for a bar, you've got "yer standard 12-bar rock boogie blues" pattern in *E*. Here's a twist you may not know, though. Try the chord forms as substitutes for Examples 25 and 26.

Aha, sort of Pete Townshendy, eh? Or remember Steppenwolf's "The Pusher" tune? Chord forms like this are, to borrow a phrase, meaty, beaty, big, and bouncy. They are what the doctor ordered for solitary guitarists cranking out rhythm chords in a power trio setting, because they're fat, and those open strings fill out the tunes. That's why guitarists like Alex Lifeson, Townshend, myself, and Jimmy Page (like the way I choose my company?) love the keys of *E, A,* and *D*—for the open strings!

Guitar Player, May 1984.

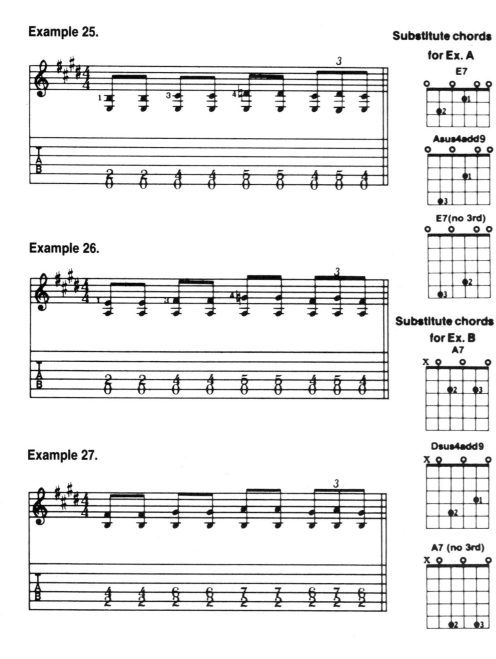

Example 25.

Example 26.

Example 27.

Substitute chords for Ex. A
E7
Asus4add9
E7(no 3rd)

Substitute chords for Ex. B
A7
Dsus4add9
A7 (no 3rd)

Example 28.   Example 29.   Example 30.   Example 31.   Example 32.

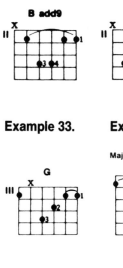

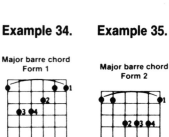

Example 33.   Example 34.   Example 35.   Example 36.   Example 37.

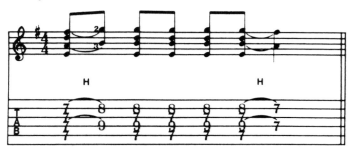

Example 38.

Example 39.

Example 28 is an add9, a thick, interesting chord to substitute for ordinary boring major chords. I also like forms that make open strings pedal tones (sustained underlying notes) and/or suspensions, as shown in Examples 29, 30, and 31.

I know that classical players gasp and die when they see ham-handed rockers playing skinny-necked axes with a strangle technique using their thumb for the bass in chord forms such as the sus4 in Example 32 that resolves to the major of Example 33. (Note: The thumb also helps mute the *A* string.) This is one way to finger the chord head in "Pinball Wizard." My opinion here is that it *works* very effectively, so it's acceptable (and some jazzers would agree, especially Tal Farlow). However, as I have said in the past, dexterity, mobility, and fingering speed are usually aided greatly by keeping the left thumb low, centered on the neck behind the fingerboard, not above it. Bend your left wrist down and *away* from you, and not up towards you. While we're on the subject, I might as well add that wearing the guitar strapped down against the thighs a la Jimmy Page might look really cool, but it is an idiosyncratic style that devastates general technique. Your average human being benefits from wearing the guitar stomach/chest high, as do Messrs. Howe, Holdsworth, Di Meola, and others.

A whole new world opened up for me on the fingerboard when I progressed from the major barre chord forms of Examples 34 and 35, and learned the different major chord forms of Examples 36 and 37. And here's why: That 1st finger, half-barring the fourth through first strings, is physically anchored so that your other three fingers can learn to dance around the position with independence and, whenever you want it or need it, there's that home key major triad (the *D, G,* and *B* strings) waiting, nice and solid. Here's what I'm talking about: Take Example 36, remove your 3rd and 2nd fingers, and strum the *D, G,* and *B* strings. Then hammer back on your 3rd and 2nd fingers. And with Example 37, you can hammer on the 3rd finger, then use it across, fretting on the *D* or *G* strings. Use your 2nd finger hammering on the fret above your 1st finger. Just keep experimenting, playing the two or three strings at a time, and hammering on or lifting off different fingers or even combinations of fingers. Then try Example 35, a *Bm11* to *Em7* Doobie Brothers/"Long Train Runnin'" lick, and Example 39 in *G*—a trademark Hendrix/"Wind Cries Mary" lick.

By Rik Emmett

Building Songs With Moving Chord Forms

Guitar Player, June 1984.

Here are some of examples based on the concept of a sliding, unchanging chord form. You'll note that I lean towards *old* wave classics on occasion: I'm catering to the nostalgic, familiar, wide-open demographic in us all.

Let's do the time warp back to 1970's *The Yes Album*, and Steve Howe's "Wurm" section of the song "Starship Trooper." Now take the well-known first-position C major chord and make two alterations to it (see Example 40), adding a G note (the chord's 5th) on top with the 4th finger at the 3rd fret on the E, or first, string. Shift the 3rd finger directly across from the C note (3rd fret, fifth string) to the alternate bass of a C chord, the G note (3rd fret, sixth string). If you slide this chord form up the neck to the eighth (VIII) position—with your 1st finger at the 8th fret—you've got a G/D (G chord, D bass note), the first chord of Steve's progression. Slide back to the fourth position (IV) for an Eb/Bb chord, and slide down again to the original first-position C/G, and you have the three chords of the progression.

Who remembers "I Can See For Miles," and Pete Townshend sliding a first-position E chord (Example 41) up three frets to create G6/E (Example 3), and then two more frets to an Aadd9/E (Example 43), to compose the powerful, ringing progression (open E and B strings, open low-E pedal tone)? Or in a more recent memory, there's Alex Lifeson of Rush sliding that same E chord up two frets to create the elegant down-tempo opening verse changes in "Xanadu."

Next I'd like to direct you to the bridge of Triumph's "Magic Power," where a first-position D chord (Example 44) slides up to the 5th fret (F/D), then the 7th, then the 10th, and finally the 12th; and then it goes (by fret position) 2 5 7 5 7 9 10 12 14. All of this just shows that one chord form goes a long way and, because of the very nature of the guitar, can function in many different roles. One more example of this versatility: Go back to that first-position E chord form, and slide it up one fret, then to the 4th, then back two, and return to the original position. The E F G F E sequence is very Spanish (Phrygian mode) in flavor and the basic progression of classics such as "Malaguena." See what I mean about versatility?

One complaint I hear most often is, "I'm stuck in a rut," or "My band's jamming is stale and limited." Well, let me suggest some classic chord progressions that provide the basis for hundreds of popular tunes, as well as some interesting changes for jams or solos. Keep in mind that inspired improvisation is not the sole territory of the soloist, but that it relies equally on the accompaniment, feel, groove, chord changes, color, and texture that surround the lead instrument.

If you've absorbed the blues progression and the function of tonic, subdominant, and dominant chords, then you've got a good start on the music of Western civilization. In the key of E, you can play songs like "Louie, Louie" with E, A, and B chords; in C, you can play "Hang On Sloopy" with C, F, and G; or you can even play "Wild Thing," say, in G, with G, C, and D. Shoot, if you figure out the right inversions (different ways of ordering a chord's notes), you could actually play the intro to Richard Strauss' *Also Sprach Zarathustra* (you know—the theme from *2001*), which is an intentional, monumental tribute to the basic power of these chords. A three-chord tune of more recent note is UB40's reggae-ish remake of "Red Red Wine," and Rush fans should recognize the I IV V as the first chordal theme in "La Villa Strangiato."

Another common three-chord progression besides the I IV V is I bVII (functionally, a IV chord of the IV chord) IV. Domenic Troiano refers to it as the "money chords": This is a slightly heavier rock and roll version of a three-chord progression, and some examples include Bad Company's "Can't Get Enough Of Your Love" in the key of C (C Bb F), or the chorus of Free's "All Right Now" in the key of A (A G D A).

You can hear this progression as the triplet accent at the end of Led Zep's "How Many More Times" in the key of E (D D D A A A E), or as the verse changes in the Who's classic "Won't Get Fooled Again" in G (G F F C). The guitar solo that follows the bridge of "Magic Power" is in the key of D over a D C G progression. This chord pattern is probably the most widely exploited in pop music, going back to tunes such as "Gloria," "Dirty Water," and the Stones' "The Last Time," right up to Van Halen's verse heads in "Panama" or AC/DC's "Back In Black." No wonder Dom calls them money chords.

Another timeless progression can be heard in "Stray Cat Strut." In *A* minor, it is *Am G F E*. It also formed the basis for the Eurythmics "Sweet Dreams." Its distinctly Spanish flavor crops up as an improvisatory base in pieces such as Al Di Meola's "Mediterranean Sundance," and might be remembered as the bed track of the old Zager & Evans tune, "In The Year 2525," or even further back as the first verse line under the Ventures' "Walk—Don't Run." In *E* minor, the progression is *Em D C B*. The last chord is usually a dominant 7th. Check it out. You'll be singing the verse from "Runaway" like Del Shannon before you know it.

Example 40.

Example 41.

Example 42.   **Example 43.**   **Example 44.**

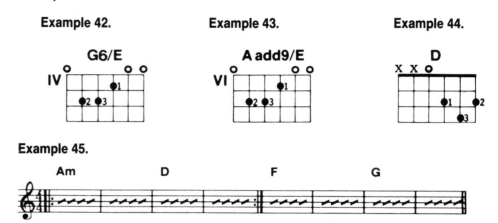

Example 45.

It's always nice to blow a little over simple, repeating chord changes such as *Em* to *A*. This can be like the verse heads of George Harrison's "My Sweet Lord," Pink Floyd's "Breathe," or even Santana's "Evil Ways." This can be nice for stretching out a little, playing two bars on each chord, and substituting altered chords for straight majors and minors. For example, in *A* minor, you could play *Am7* to *D9*, or *Am9* to *D7*. Sometimes when I jam on this change, I turn it around with the chords in Example 45. You can repeat the *Am* to *D* as often as you like before you use the *F* and *G* to turn it around again. (And an *Fmaj7* sounds nice as a substitute for the straight *F* major.)

Sometimes two chords that at first glance don't seem to relate can provide an interesting background for a solo. Pat Metheny's "Phase Dance" exploits an interesting *Bm* to *F* tonality a fair bit, and the intros to Def Leppard's "Foolin'" and Heart's "Crazy On You" use an *Am* to *F* change with great success.

Here's a discography for those who want to check out some of the songs and albums mentioned in this article. Yes, "Starship Trooper," *The Yes Album*, Atlantic, 19131; the Who, "I Can See For Miles," *Meaty, Beaty, Big & Bouncy*, MCA, 37001, and "Won't Get Fooled Again," *Who's Next*, 37217; Rush, "Xanadu," *Farewell To Kings*, Mercury, SRM-1-1184, and "La Villa Strangiato," *Hemispheres*, SRM-1-3743; Triumph, "Magic Power," *Allied Forces*, Victor AFL1-3902; the Kingsmen, "Louie, Louie," *The Best Of The Kingsmen*, Rhino [1201 Olympic Blvd., Santa Monica, CA 90404], 605; the McCoys, "Hang On Sloopy," *More American Graffiti*, MCA, 2-6009; UB40, "Red Red Wine," *Labor Of Love*, A&M, 6-4980.

Bad Company, "Can't Get Enough (Of Your Love)," *Bad Company*, Swan Song, 8501; Free, "All Right Now," *Fire & Water*, A&M, 3126; Led Zeppelin, "How Many More Times," *Led Zeppelin*, Atlantic, 19126; Rolling Stones, "Sympathy For The Devil," *Beggars Banquet*, London, PS-539 and "The Last Time," *Big Hits*, NPS-1; Them, "Gloria," *Them—Featuring Van Morrison*. London, 71053-54; Van Halen, "Panama," *1984*, Warner Bros., 1-23985; AC/DC, "Back In Black," *Back In Black*, Atlantic, 16018; Stray Cats, "Stray Cat Strut," *Built For Speed*, EMI, ST 17070: Eurythmics, "Sweet Dreams," *Sweet Dreams*, Victor, AFL1-4681; Al Di Meola, "Mediterranean Sundance," *Elegant Gypsy*, Columbia, 34461; the Ventures, "Walk—Don't Run," *Very Best Of The Ventures*, Liberty, LN 10122; Del Shannon, "Runaway," *At The Hop*, MCA, AA 1111; George Harrison, "My Sweet Lord," *All Things Must Pass*, Capitol, STCH 639; Pink Floyd, "Breathe," *Dark Side Of The Moon*, Harvest, 11163; Santana, "Evil Ways," Columbia, PC9781; Pat Metheny, "Phase Dance," *Pat Metheny*, ECM, 1-1114; Def Leppard, "Foolin'," *Pyromania*, Mercury, 422-810308-M M1; Heart, "Crazy On You," *Heart's Greatest Hits/Live*, Epic, KE2-36888.

By Rik Emmett

Playing And Singing At The Same Time

Guitar Player, September 1985.

Contrary to popular belief, some things are a little tougher and more complex than walking and chewing gum simultaneously. Just as learning to play the guitar requires the development of coordination between independent tasks—those of each hand and, ultimately, each finger of each hand—so does accompanying your own singing. You have added another element to your performing process, and must come to terms with the fact that it compromises the sublimity of the two disciplines. For myself, it is usually a case of learning the guitar part until it's stone-cold, embedded as an unconscious, autonomic function. Let's call this "Blind Memorization"—no peeking! Even then, I sometimes have to tap my foot, pump my leg, and shake my booty, as it were. (In the same way, a drummer might maintain one "steady time" limb, while the other three go polyrhythmic: Body language keeps it all together, while he or she consciously concentrates on the thickest, "top" element of the layering process.) Then I must concentrate completely on the vocal line's rhythms and accents. Helpful hint: For your foot taps, figure out which subdivision of the "count" makes it easier for you to sing your melody line—eighths, quarters, or half-notes.

On the extremely rare occasion (hack, cough) that I cannot manage a guitar part under a vocal, I try to keep the *vocal* melody and phrasing as close to the original as possible, and rearrange the accompanying guitar part. I try, at least, to keep the *changes* in the right places. I use techniques of muting, resting, and stroking fewer strings to make a part more sparse (and manageable), and sometimes I employ that time-worn musical practice: Faking.

When accompanying yourself, try to minimize awkward chord forms and long positional shifts. This requires a thorough knowledge of inversions of chords in different forms and positions all over the neck. Then, by employing a technique I call "blind guide finger" changing, you can make all your left-hand chord fingerings without looking or thinking about them, and concentrate on the vocal.

The "blind guide finger" technique goes something like this. You're playing an *Am* in the first position (Example 46), and you've got to go to a *G* (Example 47), but it seems an insurmountable problem because you can't look at it. And you *can't* take your yapper away from the microphone because you're singing an emotional, flowing legato line.

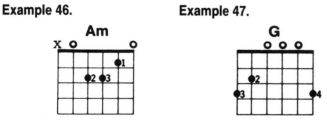

Example 46. **Example 47.**

What will you do?

Solution: Isolate the 3rd-finger move from the 2nd fret of the *G* string to the 3rd fret of the big *E* string. Make that move one of pure "blind memorization" and alter your strumming to pick that low *G* note on the change. On the next beat of the bar, you could strum just the open strings. Then on the third beat of the bar, you could fold the 2nd and 4th fingers in and upstroke through all of the strings (Example 48).

Example 48.

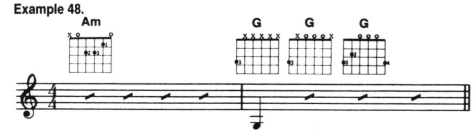

Now let me give you an example of how inversions and forms in one position can make life easier. Let's say you're in the key of *G*, and you have to play an *Eb* to *F* to *G* progression (Example 49). Your barre never moves: It allows you, through some practice and blind guide finger manipulation, to make the changes without looking for different neck positions.

Example 49.

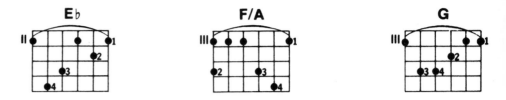

If a chord or form is presenting an awkward problem, you might also alter the right-hand strumming or picking to allow you to strike an open string or an easy-to-grab first-position chord form.

Another way to ensure that you'll be able to handle playing and singing at the same time is to compose the song that way. it sounds simple enough, but a lot of writing and song construction takes place away from the guitar (in your head, on the written page, at a keyboard). Nowadays, more and more songs are written and recorded in a multi-track piecemeal fashion. and performers don't find out whether they can handle their parts at once until they go into tour rehearsals.

There is an extremely high level of guitar skill sublimated in the work of "traditional" singer/songwriters such as Paul Simon, Bruce Cockburn, and James Taylor (some of my personal favorites). You could do a lot worse than trying to emulate their fingerstyle accompaniment chops.

Example 50 shows a simple, standard broken-arpeggio fingerpicking style pattern for vocal accompaniment. Option A shows how you could play it with a flatpick and one, two, or three right-hand fingers. Option B is the standard, "by the book" thumb-and-three-fingers approach, while option C, I'm slightly abashed to admit, is the most natural way I seem to be able to get the job done.

Example 50.

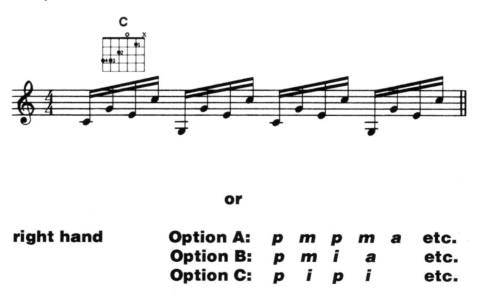

or

right hand						
Option A:	*p*	*m*	*p*	*m*	*a*	etc.
Option B:	*p*	*m*	*i*	*a*		etc.
Option C:	*p*	*i*	*p*	*i*		etc.

Even though I noted earlier that simultaneous playing and singing puts its restrictions on both pursuits, it can also provide a unique and sympathetic interpretation of a song, as the two disciplines emanate from one source. And unless you're an unrehearsed schizo, what could be tighter?

By Rik Emmett

Hot Memphis Rhythm

I'd like to address one of the most common topics requested by guitarists: The Memphis-style R&B rhythms made so popular by players such as Steve Cropper and Cornell Dupree.

The most identifiable part of this style is its combination of funky rhythms with occasional two- or three-note fills thrown in for some spice. This dual demand on the right hand requires a good, loose, playing approach, as well as a neat left-hand damping technique. Many of the licks often involve either a one-finger slide of a two- or three-note chord, or a bend. We'll deal with both of these in this lesson.

First, let's just concentrate on the licks themselves shown in Example 51, so you can get a clear idea of just the sound you want to get across. This also gives you a chance to practice the necessary damping, so play them as if they're part of the overall rhythm, with a strong right-hand approach over all the strings.

Once you've got that fairly well down, combine the lead and rhythm together. Remember that the bulk of the playing consists of the rhythm part, and that the lead work acts mainly as punctuation, or accents to the overall rhythm pattern. You'll note that in Example 52, we make use of both types of fills: the two-note licks with bends, and the chordal slides. Remember to keep it funky and smooth at the same time.

By Arlen Roth

Guitar Player, June 1988.

Example 51.

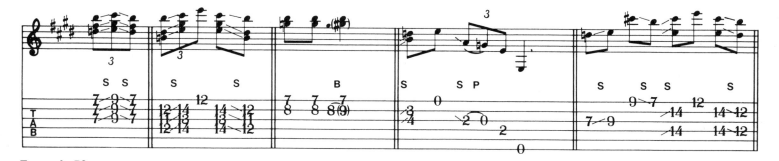

Example 52. E9

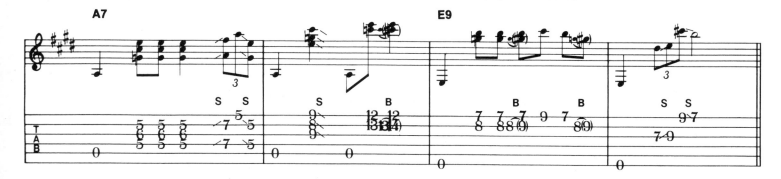

Chapter 3:
Rock Techniques

Vibrato

Guitar Player, January 1986.

I've limited this piece to left-hand (fretting-hand) vibrato. But keep in mind that "vibrato" is also used to denote pitch changes brought about by tailpiece or whammy-bar devices, electronic modulation of pitch or volume (a feature of some old tube amps, Fender Rhodes pianos, and electronic Leslie-like devices), and Doppler-effect pitch and volume changes, afforded by rotating deflectors and Leslie-style speakers.

Why use vibrato? Because it can make a note, double-stop, or chord sound better, as long as it's not overused. Once mastered, vibrato adds warmth, tone, and sustain without the use of effects devices. There are several types of vibrato: Finger, whole-hand, pivoting-hand, classical-style, and arm. Whatever type you happen to be using, it's important to be able to control its amount and speed.

Finger Vibrato

Finger vibrato requires moving one or more fingers perpendicular to the string while the hand remains stationary. The only time I use this is when I'm playing a chord with a melody note that needs vibrato without affecting the other chordal tones. Finger vibrato is a good way to bring out a melody that is not the highest note of the chord and wouldn't stand out on its own. Of course, you must commit one finger for that note; you can't barre two or three strings and single-out one for vibrato. A minority of players use this technique for most or all of their vibrato.

Whole-Hand Vibrato

Whole-hand vibrato involves using the entire hand, without a pivot point. The hand just moves up and down (perpendicular to the neck), sometimes with the thumb supporting on the neck. I find this difficult to control, but it has the advantage of enabling you to keep your thumb behind the neck, rather than around it.

I call my style of vibrato *pivoting-hand vibrato*. The basic idea is to touch the back of the neck with the point of your left hand, as shown in Figure 1.

Figure 1.

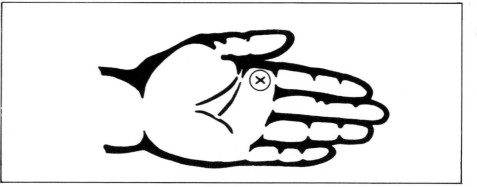

I also anchor my left hand by reaching around with the thumb, as shown in Figure 2. This enables you to have the best leverage for bending and vibrato in the upwards direction (toward the ceiling), and to have your hand acting as a counterweight for downward bends (toward the floor) and vibrato. Your wrist is the part that provides the energy, and the vibrato is easy to control, due to the fairly natural twisting force involved and the leverage at the pivot point.

Classical-Style Vibrato

This type of vibrato works best on nylon strings, since they are more elastic than steel. However, it can be used to some extent on the electric guitar, as long as you stay near the center of the string length, where it is most effective. The basic idea is to move your hand back and forth (parallel to the string, rather than perpendicular) while holding

Previous page: Yngwie Malmsteen.

the note or notes (see Figure 3). The movement is similar to a violinist's vibrato, and your fingers push and pull on the string in a lengthwise fashion, instead of deflecting the string from a straight line, which increases the tension. When your finger applies pressure towards the bridge, tension is momentarily decreased on the sounding portion of the string, resulting in a definite lowering of pitch. Applying pressure toward the nut increases the tension on the sounding portion of the string, with an increase in pitch.

One important distinction of classical-type vibrato is that it is the only one that raises *and* lowers the pitch of the fretted note. The pitch that your ear hears averages out to the same as the fretted note, which makes it very appropriate for delicate tuning, chords, and any part that is extremely pitch-sensitive.

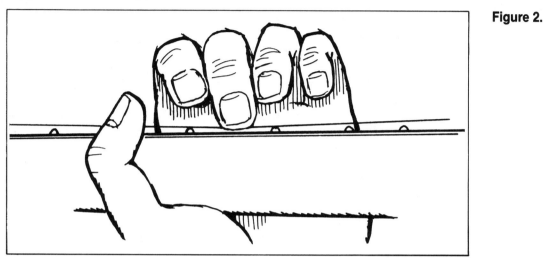

Figure 2.

Figure 3.

Arm Vibrato

This is a severe type of vibrato that I use occasionally. It is very hard for me to control the speed of this vibrato because it requires an almost spastic arm movement. Your finger, hand, and wrist are held rigid, with your thumb clear of the neck. The vibrato comes from an overly fast up-and-down movement at the elbow. Like I said before, it is fairly radical and should be used sparingly.

To summarize, here are a few general guidelines to keep in mind. All vibratos (except the classical-type) bend the string and cause it to be momentarily *sharp*. In most cases, if your guitar is in tune, non-classical vibratos sound fine, since the note keeps returning to the correct pitch. Obviously, the more you bend, the more drastic the pitch change, so be able to control the amount of vibrato to fit the situation.

In addition, learn to control the speed of the vibrato, which is critical to expressiveness of the technique. While vibratoing, practice both bending up (toward the ceiling) and bending down (toward the floor), and do it with each finger, and on each string. You will be able to bend the *E* strings *away* from the edge of the fingerboard only.

Remember: Bends, vibrato, and attack changes are what keep us from being replaced by sampling keyboards, so stick with it. Good luck.

By Steve Morse

Damping And Muting

Guitar Player, October 1986.

In dictionary definitions and common usage, the terms *damp* and *mute* seem interchangeable, sometimes referring to a muffling, softening of tone and vibration, other times referring to an out-and-out "extinguishing" of oscillation and vibration. Personally—and for clarity—I will refer to the deadening of a string so that it doesn't sound at all as *muting*, and to the muffling of a string so that it has little or no sustain as *damping*.

To be perfectly honest, this is an aspect of my own playing that tends to be much more subconscious than conscious, which is to say that I hardly ever analyze sections of music that I'm playing, trying to figure out the hows, wheres, and whens of damping and muting. I guess that naturally evolves out of my efforts to play the notes of the part correctly and get it to sound right, letting necessity be the mother of invention. Basically, I use the back outside edge of my right palm to mute, damp, and stop strings. Sometimes after a downstroke or strum, I rotate my right wrist through and damp with the muscle-pad below the thumb on the *other* side of the palm. In some instances, my 1st finger on the left hand rests across the treble-side strings (mostly on the *E*, or first) to keep them silent during passages. But what it really boils down to is a continuous coordination between the attack (left-hand finger), and the damp (soft finger stop by left-hand fingers and/or the backside fleshy muscle of the right-hand palm).

If a picture is worth a thousand words, then let's save each other a lot of writing and reading and let the camera do most of the work.

Figure 4 shows a full damp by the right-hand backside muscle of the palm. This is the most common method of damping, and is used extensively (especially on electric guitar) for a chunky pick attack with no sustain. It's perfect for Al Di Meola staccato-style running of notes or for that Chuck Berry two-string rhythm chording that has also evolved into a heavy metal power-fifth chord style of rhythm playing.

Figure 5 shows a common right-hand position for lead playing on "inside" strings (the *D*, *G*, and *B*). Notice how the picking hand has flattened out and the fleshy muscle-pad below the thumb rests against the bass strings to keep them from vibrating, while the second and third fingers have curled around to deaden the first string. This hand position uses the "front" edge of the pick to downstroke the string.

Figure 4.   **Figure 5.**

If I were to play on the low *A* or *E* strings (and sometimes the *D*) my right wrist would curl around to release the damp on the bass strings, and the right hand would rest with the back edge of the hand across the treble side, as in Figure 6. Notice how the third finger still rests anchored and curled against the first string and the "back" edge of the pick provides the downstroke.

Figure 7 shows a different fingerstyle-and-pick technique, and consequently a different muting approach. The outside edge of the right thumb mutes on the bass strings, and the second, third, and fourth fingers of the right hand rest, anchor, and mute the treble-side *G, B,* and *E* strings, respectively. Figure 8 demonstrates a pickless approach, but the idea is more or less the same. These are both primarily hand positions that favor chording and broken-chording (arpeggiating) passages, but some jazz and rock players exploit them for other things, as well.

Figure 6.

Figure 7.

Figure 8.

Here are a few types of muting: A rest stroke (up or down), where you pick through a string and come to rest against an adjacent string, is an effective method of muting a noisy neighbor—in this case, with your *pick*.

The concept behind the wide fingerspread of Figure 9's full-hand mute is to eliminate any unwanted harmonic overtones. A casual one-finger mute across the strings at certain places may not kill the string vibration completely, but will merely divide the oscillation proportionately, creating an overtone. Widespread soft pressure ensures that *all* oscillation stops.

Figure 9.

Figure 10 is perhaps the most common mute of all—where the fleshy pad of the finger that's fretting a note leans over and rests against an adjacent string to deaden it. A lot of times on chord diagrams such as Example 1's, you see an "X" over an "inside" string. Figure 10 shows how you mute that string.

Figure 10.

Example 1.

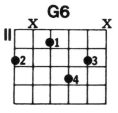

Figure 11 is a good example of that "subconscious" natural evolution of muting I alluded to previously. Good left-hand positional fingering leads you towards maintaining a natural, four-fret spread with the four fingers of the left hand. So if fingers 2, 3, or 4 are busy doing something, but 1 can rest, it can do so in a useful fashion by laying across some unwanted strings *behind* the action and muting them.

Once you've developed some experience on guitar, you sort of subconsciously keep that 1st finger resting against the first string when you're not using either party (Figure 12), just as you don't really think about the fact that your thumb is rotating up and over the top edge of the fingerboard to mute the sixth string for such things as the very common *C* chord of Figure 13 and Example 2.

Figure 11.

Figure 12.

Figure 13.

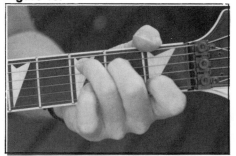

Example 2.

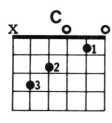

Before I sign off, let me remind you that there is no right or wrong way to get the job done. These examples are just a few personal suggestions, which may seem perfectly sensible to you, or completely lunar. In any case, I offer these as a basic foundation upon which you may build and progress. As you develop, your need for more techniques will lead you to fresh discoveries and personal creative invention.

Keep in mind that some of the subtlest, trickiest things that a conscientious musician is always learning are the hows, whens, wheres, and whys . . . of silence.

By Rik Emmett

Harmonics And The Whammy Bar

Amidst today's plethora of whammy shakers and harmonic makers, Brad Gillis stands as a man with a style of his own. Here he shares some of his most distinctive tricks with you.

Certain keys are better than others for playing harmonics. For things such as "(You Can Still) Rock In America" [*Midnight Madness*], which is in *A*, I hit the harmonics above the 4th fret on the *A* string and the 5th fret on the *D* and *G* strings (Figure 14). This gives you the major third, perfect fourth, and minor seventh. I use the whammy bar to create vibrato and the dive effect.

Guitar Player, **November 1986.**

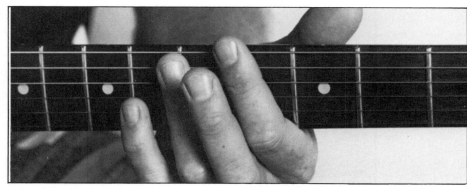

Figure 14.

I use the same technique in "Touch Of Madness" [*Midnight Madness*]. Since it's in the key of *E*, I play the same pattern transposed down one string. So I hit the harmonics above the 4th fret on the low *E* and the 5th fret on the *A* and *D* strings (Figure 15).

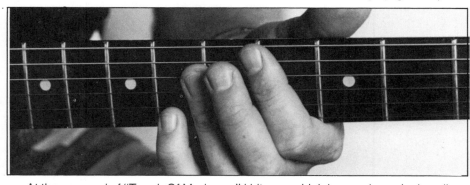

Figure 15.

At the very end of "Touch Of Madness," I hit a very high harmonic squiggle pull-up. This uses three harmonics on the *G* string. It goes from low to high, so first I hit the harmonic above the 7th fret, and then the ones above the 5th and 3rd frets. I have the tremolo bar depressed as I hit each note, and shake it as I raise the pitch (Figure 16). If you run the notes into each other with enough volume, you can't hear when the pick hits. It sounds like one note.

Figure 16.

In the key of A, the highest harmonic that I've been able to get is the high A that's found slightly behind the 2nd fret on the G string (Figure 17). (Using the bar, you can bring it up even further to a major third—in this case, C#.)

Figure 17.

With the bar pushed down, you hit the octave harmonic above the 12th fret on the G string (Figure 18). Pull the note up as high as you want with the bar. Then use a left-hand finger to tap—don't pick—above the 12th, 7th, or 5th frets, and bring it down.

Figure 18.

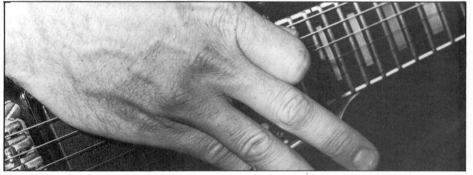

I use another tap at the start of the solo in "Sister Christian" [*Midnight Madness*]. After the fifth note, I play a C on the A string, tap the note 12 frets higher at the 15th fret, and pull up with the bar. My 4th finger hits at the 5th fret on the D string, the pulled-up bar turns that G note into an A. Then I release the bar back down to its original level to drop that note to a G (Figure 19).

Figure 19.

Later on in the "Sister Christian" solo, I use three fingers to bend the high E string at the 10th fret from D to E, and then tap at the 13th fret (Figure 20). The second bend is a half-step (Eb), and I tap on the 16th fret.

Figure 20.

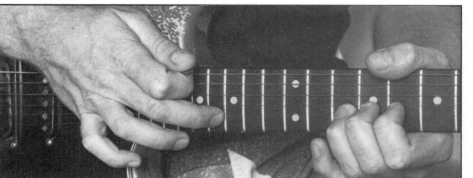

Hitting the *E* and *A* strings above the 3rd fret gives you a high harmonic fifth and a root above that (Figure 21). You can create a cool effect by bringing this up with the bar to a root and major third.

Figure 21.

The first high harmonic in the "Don't Tell Me You Love Me" solo [*Dawn Patrol*] is done by striking the string with the pick and the flesh of the thumb at the same time. The placement of the thumb along the pick is critical for these types of pick bites, and I always use a metal Jim Dunlop pick (Figure 22).

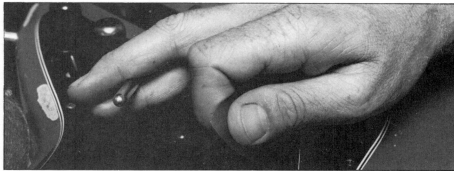

Figure 22.

About five-eighths of the way through the "Don't Tell Me You Love Me" solo, I go up to the *B* at the 19th fret on the high *E* string and create a flutter. There are two ways of doing this. First, you can use the middle finger of your right hand to flick the end of the tremolo, causing it to warble (Figure 23). The other way to cause it to warble is to just hit the body of the guitar, which shakes the tremolo (Figure 24).

Figure 23.

Figure 24.

When you move the string with just finger vibrato, you can only *raise* the pitch (Figure 25). You get a smoother note texture if you use the bar to go under it and over it slightly. This means your pitch will be right in the center of your pull. Figure 26 shows another trick where you add finger vibrato and use the bar to go down to any note you want.

Figure 25.

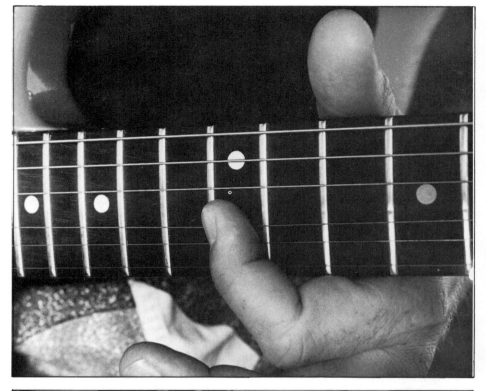

Figure 26.

The technique in Figure 27 is a good attention-getter for the beginning or end of a solo. I start by having the bar pressed down low in my right hand. I hit any note and start bringing it up with the bar. My left hand reaches over to grab the bar and keep it going up, while my right hand taps my low *E* string against the pickup.

Figure 27.

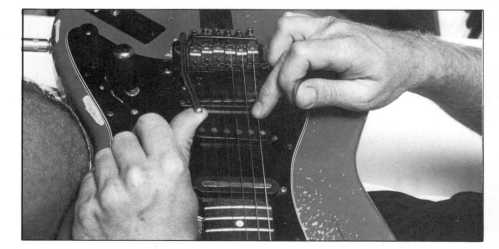

I end a lot of my solos with harmonic pull-ups. For these, the bar is depressed before I strike the note (Figure 28). For instance, I end "Sentimental Street" [*7 Wishes*] by doing this with the harmonic above the 3rd fret on the G string. After I strike the harmonic, I use the bar to pull the note up to a very high G harmonic.

Figure 28.

My Floyd Rose doesn't have the fine tuners, so by resting my palm on the back of the tremolo, I can push down to get sharp note tremolo (Figure 29).

Figure 29.

For the harmonics in the intro to "Seven Wishes," I mute the low E string with my right-hand palm and get a real hard, crunchy lead sound. Then, as I run my left-hand 3rd finger between the 2nd and 3rd frets of the string to pull out harmonics, I demute. After that, I go up to the harmonics above the 7th fret on the E and A strings and use the bar (Figure 30).

Figure 30.

Everyone wants to own a Ferrari these days, and here's how you get a guitar to sound like one. With the volume off, hit the harmonics above the 9th fret on the E and A strings. Bring your left hand over to the bar, pull it down, and then bring it up as you roll on the volume with your right hand (Figure 31).

Figure 31.

By Brad Gillis
As told to Jas Obrecht

String Bending Techniques

Guitar Player, February 1983.

Combining String Bending With Single-Note Work

Let's look at something rarely discussed, but absolutely essential to all types of lead playing—the technique of getting in and getting out of a bending position. This skill is essential to developing the emotional content of one's lead work.

The Bending Position. While many jazz stylists employ very subtle bends, most rock and blues players desire a more radical effect, bending a note up a half-step, a whole-step, or even more. In such cases, the fingers alone are not enough. The left *hand* itself must be totally committed to the bending process.

There are two factors that go into this left-hand commitment. First, your thumb *should* come up over the edge of the fingerboard to give some opposing pressure for the bend to work against; second, you should place any other available fingers *behind* the bend to help it along and to push the other strings out of the way. When bending a string down, away from you, the thumb over the fingerboard can still be useful, but it is not as crucial. As you make the bend, your hand should pivot from the point where the base of the 1st finger presses against the side of the neck.

Getting Out. Normally, getting out of a bend presents little difficulty. But sometimes a finger tied up in pushing a string will be needed elsewhere for normal fretting, In that case, remove the finger you need while the remaining fingers reinforce the bent note enough to keep it from losing its pitch prematurely. Let's say, for instance, that the 1st, 2nd, and 3rd fingers are involved when you need the 1st finger to play a note on another string. While the 1st finger moves, the 2nd and 3rd fingers remain in firm control of the bent string, and can still sustain, release, or alter the note in any way desired.

The rock/blues solo I've written out in Example 3 contains several situations calling for sustaining the bend while moving another finger. You should probably do a little experimenting to see whether the 2nd or 3rd finger would be more comfortable in each

Example 3.

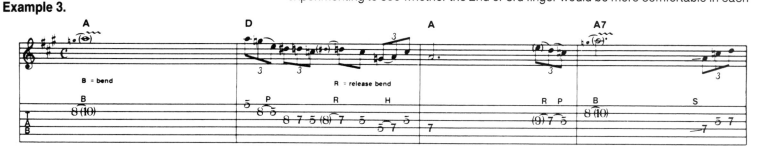

situation. I know that if I must make a completely independent bend, especially at the start of a lick, I'll always go to the three-finger position. If the bend occurs more *during* the course of a lick, I'm often forced to go to the slightly weaker two-finger approach. (Notes in parentheses are reached by either bending or releasing the previous tone.) Again, you should try each case a few different ways to see which is the best suited for you.

Combining Bends With Stretches

Over the years I've come up with a lot of interesting positions on the neck that combine the use of bends with other fretted notes involving rather extreme stretches. The stretches themselves aren't so difficult, but they are made so because a great deal of the hand is committed to making the bend possible, leaving very little in the way of true flexibility for the hand's muscles. This combination of bending and stretching is a great tool to have, and it's certainly a fine exercise for getting your left hand in better shape.

The important thing to keep in mind while practicing these bends is that you still must use another finger behind the bending finger to help the bend along. This at first may seem to tie your hand up too much, but in actuality it's making it easier for you to execute the lick than by keeping the pitch up with one finger. The addition of having to stretch another note would even further weaken the one-finger bend. Of course, another great thing about this technique is that it gives you some intriguing harmonies and positions usually thought impossible when bending.

Example 4 includes a group of licks utilizing this technique. Some require the bend and the stretched note to be sustained together, while at other times you need only to catch the stretched note momentarily, not putting as much strain on your fretting hand.

These licks only represent a small part of what you can do with this technique, so feel free to try some of your own outlandish ideas. You never know what will happen.

Example 4.

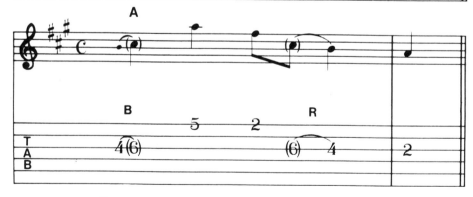

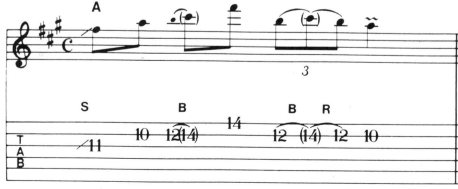

Example 4 (continued).

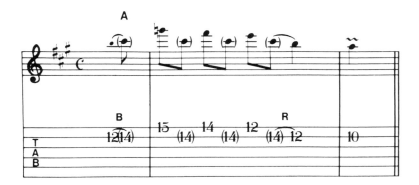

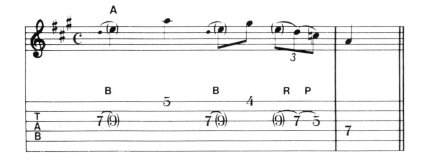

Harmonics And The Whammy Bar

Combining string bending with partial barre forms, the lead guitarist can produce a variety of exciting licks. What does this hybrid technique have going for it? Well, the barre creates a firm platform from which a great many hammer-ons and pulls-offs can be executed, and—if you pick properly—you can make many of these licks rather fast and flashy sounding.

Now, the act of getting in and out of a bending position is very important to the proper execution of this type of lick. This is because your left-hand fingers have a dual involvement. In order to commit the *entire* left hand to the bend, they must all push together—and yet they must be instantly available, either for fretting new notes or switching to a partial barre position. All this requires some pretty agile movement on your part and a sense of knowing where you're going ahead of time.

In Example 5, be sure to commit your entire hand to the bending process, releasing the bend just in time to use your 1st finger for the barre on the 8th fret of the first and second strings.

The next lick (Example 6) is essentially the same as the first, except that we've added a bend from *B♭* to *C* on the last note. Try to use the same three-fingered approach for both bends (back up the bending finger with two others).

In Example 7, we play a harmony note with the bend. The harmony note, a high *E♭* on the first string, 11th fret, is held by the 4th finger of the left hand. Since we are using the

Example 5. **Example 6.** **Example 7.**

left-hand 4th finger, we can still afford to invest three fingers in making a strong, clean bend.

The next two examples (8 and 9) feature the more difficult sorts of licks associated with this technique. You've probably heard similar sounds in the flashy solos and fills of people like Jimmy Page, Eric Clapton, Jeff Beck, and Jimi Hendrix. These one-bar exercises—as brief as they are—will become quite effective when you are able to play them fast and in quick repetition. The first example will not require a barre, since we're only playing one string after the bend. When you really get going at a good clip, you'll probably find it easier to use only the 2nd finger for the bend, meanwhile keeping the 1st finger firmly planted on the second string at the 8th fret.

Example 9 is rather difficult to execute cleanly, mainly because the hammer-on that crosses the first and second beats is delayed, occurring after the intervening C has sounded. In other words, the second-string G must sustain long enough to receive the hammer-on B♭ after the first string C has been plucked. Just to be sure we understand, let's analyze the fretboard events: On notes one and two of the third beat, pick the third-string F and bend it up to G and allow it to ring as you go into the triplet. On the first note of the triplet, pick the first-string C, and on the *second* note, hammer-on B♭ from the still-ringing G on the second string. For the third note of the triplet, pull off from the 11th fret to the 8th fret. Clear? If not, try playing one note at a time, while reviewing the instructions as you go. It should click then. Once you understand the example, gradually build up speed. Once again, you'll probably find that your best bet for achieving maximum speed is a 2nd-finger bend under a firmly mounted barre.

Example 8. **Example 9.**

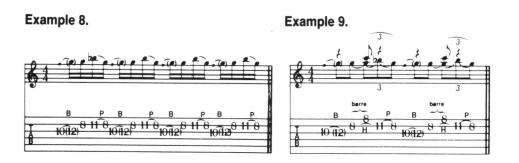

Three-Note Bends And Beyond

You all know I enjoy bending strings, but if any of you have listened to my records, you'll note the extensive use of three-, four-, and even five-note bends in my solos and backup parts. So far, I have discussed how you must stretch different strings varying distances for many two-note bends. This, however, is rarely the case when bending whole chords because the effect we want to get is more of a bend-and-return or release-of-a-bend sound.

Generally speaking, you want to look for groups of notes or chords that have nice, clustered formations that are easy to "grab." Because of this, I like to bend D and D7 forms, other 7th forms, and 9th chords. In every case, except for chords that have notes on the high E string, you should make these bends *away* from yourself. This gives you a lot more leverage, and you can grip the neck with your thumb while the rest of your hand pulls down and away in a pivoting motion.

Keep in mind that these bends are really not as difficult as they seem. As long as you can keep strength in the bend, and not let the strings overlap each other, you should be in pretty good shape. The first bend illustrated here (Example 10) is based on the 9th-chord form, and involves all four fingers of the fretting hand. First, start by playing the notes, and

Example 10.

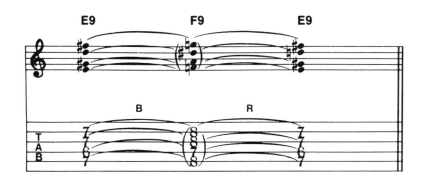

then bend them all *down*, applying even pressure to each string. Ideally, what we want is the effect of a *half-step* bend.

Next in Example 11, we take the same bend and make it part of an *E9* to *D9* change, something I like to do when reaching this part of a blues progression. Here we are first sounding the normal fretted *E9* chord, and then sneaking down one fret below it and silently bending up to something approximating the *E9*, so we can then release the bend to a *D#9* and finally *slide* that position down one fret to the *D9*.

Example 11.

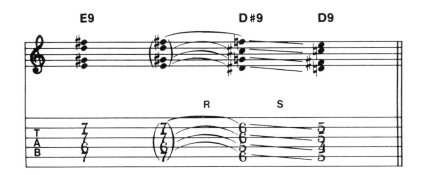

In the form of the 9th chord shown in Example 12, the same four fingers do the bending, but the turned-around position of this chord makes it just a little more difficult to get a good pivoting motion happening. Try it slowly at first, making sure to keep the strings from overlapping each other.

Example 12.

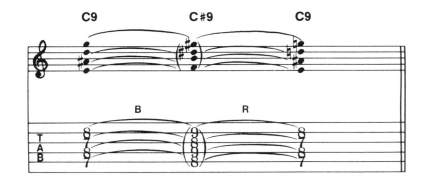

This position in Example 13 is one of my favorite discoveries because it takes one three-note chord and turns it into a completely new chord quite naturally with the bend. In this case, we are taking an *A7* position and, with the bend, actually turning it into a *D* major chord! You'll find that this kind of lick lends itself to the melodic qualities of a solo quite readily, and can be further explored by playing one note at a time with either a pick-and-finger technique or by individually picking the notes.

Example 13.

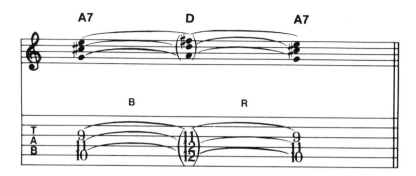

In this final, most difficult three-note bend, based on the *D* chord form (Example 14), we must bend *towards* us. This brings the chord up a whole-step, but to a *minor* form. Here, we're taking an *A* chord up to a *Bm* with the bend.

Example 14.

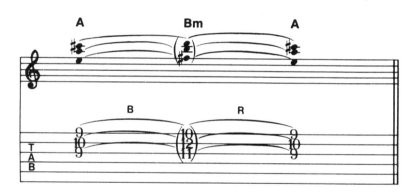

Bending On The Lower Strings

Many guitarists shy away from bending the lower strings, but there's truly a wealth of great sounds using this technique. In fact, they're often easier to execute than their high-string counterparts. Of course, when bending on the low *E, A,* and *D* strings, we must almost always bend away from us (towards the high *E* string). In the case of this kind of bend, we gain strength from the pivoting motion our hand makes as we bend down and away. We gain further strength from our thumb coming over the edge of the fingerboard and applying added pressure in the direction that counts. It also serves a bonus role of damping out any unwanted accidental tones on the lower strings that may not be involved directly with the bend.

Again, as I've often stressed, you must help the bend along with as many other fingers as are available behind the actual bending finger. This also serves the additional role as a damper of unwanted tones, particularly when the bend is released back to its "relaxed" position.

First, in Example 15, let's look at some real twangy licks that involve notes bent on the low *E* string. This string is the loosest of all, so be careful not to *overbend* as so many guitarists do when they first try these. Observe that some of the licks keep the bend up to pitch, while others use a bend and release.

The *A* string is also great for bends, but since it's a bit stiffer than the low *E*, it can present more problems. It's also crowded between two strings, unlike the low *E*, and that means that damping is even more important in this more hazardous situation. Note how some of the licks in Example 16 combine bends on both the *A* and low *E* strings.

The *D* is perhaps the most difficult string to bend on the guitar. It's got many strikes against it: It's in the middle of the fingerboard, and it's thin but still wound, which definitely makes it the tightest string to bend. (Those who have ever tried long bends on a wound *G* string know what I'm talking about!) Nevertheless it is useful, and if you can execute bends in Example 17 on this elusive string, you've got something special happening!

Example 15.

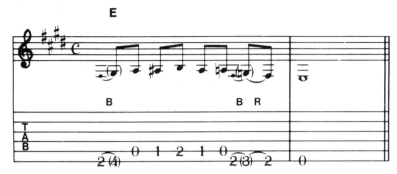

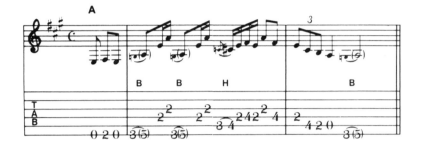

play simultaneously

Example 16.

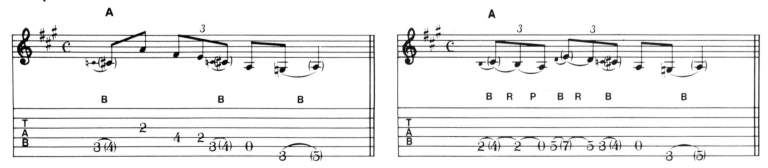

Example 17.

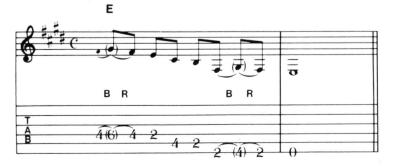

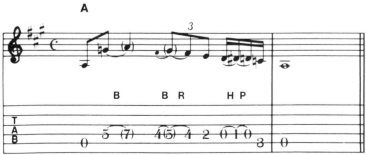

Bending In Open Positions

Obviously, when someone gets heavily into string bending, most of his experiments take place up the neck in the closed, more lead guitar-oriented positions. I've been bending strings all over the place for quite some time now, and I've also found some really nice "closed-position" bends that exist lower on the neck; these are based upon open chord positions.

One of the primary reasons why many of us stay away from open-position bends is that we think it's too hard to bend this far down the neck, that there isn't enough slack behind the string to help the bend along. Well, that's really not true, and in fact many open-position bends are very easy. Certainly where chord-like bends are concerned (in which certain other notes must be sustained over the bend itself), these positions hold a definite edge over similar "closed" positions.

In the positions notated in Example 18, you'll note my usage of the bend-release, pull-off pattern. This lends itself perfectly to the open-string positions, as we can now pull-off on a nicely ringing open string without having to create the usual "anchor" note utilized during closed pull-off licks. Most of the licks involve the major third in one way or another, such as bending up to it, or as a suspended-fourth type of bend that releases to the major third.

I hope you enjoy this selection of ideas, and that you use them to come up with some of your own ideas. Remember to use as many fingers as possible to help bend the strings, and you'll be all right!

By Arlen Roth

Example 18.

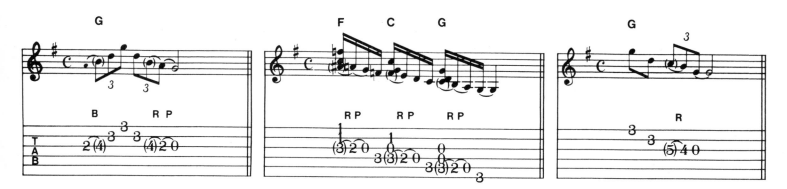

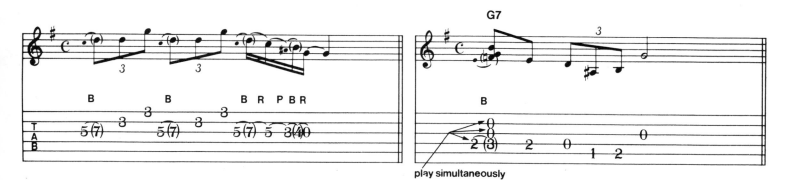

play simultaneously

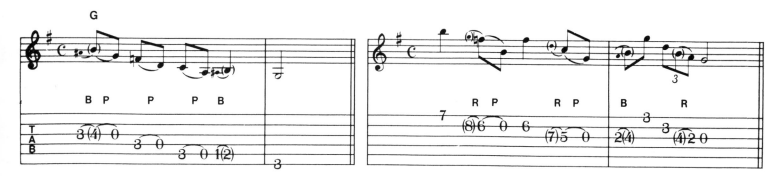

Eric Clapton's Vibrato, String Bending, And Phrasing

Guitar Player, July 1985.

While borrowing from a variety of influences, Eric Clapton always has maintained a high quality in his music. A player with deep blues roots, he manages to integrate facets of B.B. King's and Otis Rush's styles with his own highly personal approach. Regardless of the type of song he's playing, it's easy to recognize his sound. Eric's classic, unique vibrato, bending style, and phrasing are three elements that enabled him to produce some of rock guitar's most memorable lines.

The key to Clapton's vibrato (and most great rock vibratos) is left-hand *pivoting* motion. Pivoting is crucial because it enables you to vibrato as slow or as fast as you desire, giving you complete control. Figures 32 and 33 show a before/after perspective of a 1st-finger vibrato a la B.B. King, where the pivot rocks the hand so that it contacts the side of the fingerboard. When playing this type of vibrato, it is the pivot itself that makes the tip of the finger move the string. So it's the motion of the whole hand to keep in mind, rather than sending all of your energy to the tip of your finger. Note that when the pivot is in its full downward motion, your hand directly faces the guitar.

Figure 32.

Figure 33.

While Clapton's string-bending approach is much imitated, few have managed to produce his degree of emotion. The key is not only his sweeping bending sound but also his use of vibrato in tandem with some of his more extreme bends. When bending away from you, vibrato is not so hard to attain, because pivoting motion can be applied to both the vibrato and the bend (Figure 34).

Figure 34.

Roth on Clapton

On the other hand, when you bend *towards* you (Figure 35), the vibrato comes from exercising complete control over a bend/release motion to create the wavering effect. It doesn't sound too difficult, but maintaining an even pulsation and pitch is something that will take a lot of practice until you build up your hand strength.

Figure 35.

Clapton's phrasing and feeling are two of his most important stylistic elements. In the six licks shown in Example 19, I've tried to capture some of this for you. In the case of phrases that use notes at the same fret on adjacent strings, such as the 7th fret on the *G* and *D* strings, try to use rapid 3rd-finger barre. This is a technique that Eric often employs, and it helps distinguish his blues licks from those of other players. For the most part, I recommend that you mainly use a three-finger left-hand approach. Your vibrato will be better because your third finger is quite a bit stronger than your pinky (resort to your pinky only if you can't reach a particular stretch). Good luck and keep that slowhand slow! [*Ed. Note: In the first half of the first beat in the final lick (and all similar phrases), pluck the two 12s* simultaneously, *quickly bending to the 14.*]

By Arlen Roth

Example 19.

Combining Hammer-Ons And Pull-Offs

Guitar Player, January 1983.

Now on to one of the hotter elements of guitar playing—the ability to combine hammer-ons and pull-offs for added left-hand speed in lead guitar.

Often when we hear the repetitious riffing of some ear-crushing showboat, it is more likely than not the result of a heavy-handed combination of these two techniques. But while some people use them to excess, when employed tastefully they are vital parts of the repertoire of any lead player. I'll define hammers and pulls more clearly so we can all begin with the same degree of understanding.

The *hammer-on*, indicated by an arch between two notes with an "h" over it, is simply any finger "hammering-on" to a second note (on a higher fret), after the intital note is picked. The force of the hammer stroke causes a second note to be sounded—in effect giving a new life to the string. To attack the string, the hammer-on finger shouldn't be too far above the fingerboard. Using more strength within closer quarters like this increases left-hand agility and control.

The *pull-off* technique is generally the opposite of the hammer-on (note that it's indicated by an arch with a "p" over it). To play the following example, pre-position both fingers of your left hand. Pluck the G with your right hand and cause the E to sound by pulling away the finger positioned on the G as shown in Example 20. Remember that pull-offs sound stronger when you remove your finger from the fretboard at approximately a 45° angle, while slightly catching the string with your callus.

To get a better idea of what hammers and pulls should feel like together, try playing this next exercise in Example 21 using only the left hand. The second hammer-on is stronger than the other two because the hammered note is on the beat (the other hammer-ons go to offbeat notes). Other than that, maintain an even volume. This is precisely how flashy players are able to play with one hand—connecting a hammer-on to a pull-off.

Example 20.   **Example 21.**

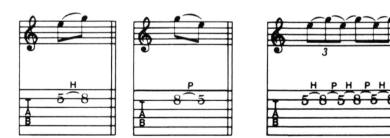

The Backtrack Scale

It's only when you start to combine other strings and move freely between them that you see the true advantages of hammer-ons and pull-offs used in tandem. This scale (see Example 22), which I often refer to as the "backtrack," uses hammers and pulls in combination while the 1st finger makes some rather rapid shifts across the strings. Why call it the backtrack scale? Though the general motion of the notes is down, there are a couple of skips back up in each measure. See if you can reverse the pattern and create an *ascending* backtrack scale.

Hammer and Pull Licks

The possibilities these techniques offer are endless. Here are some of the hotter licks that can be derived from this particular blues scale. Let's look at the next licks in Example 23 in greater detail. In the first you have a difficult leap from the E on the second string to

Example 22.

Example 23.

the *D* on the fifth string (sixth and seventh notes). Learn to make the jump quickly with the 1st finger in order to maintain the tempo. In the second lick there is a *short* barre across the first and second string only. When you come to the *D* # (a passing tone commonly added to the five-note blues scale), get the 3rd and 1st fingers ready, pinning the 7th and 5th frets while you're picking the 8th fret *D* #. Be sure to change your time feeling to two notes to the beat instead of three when you come to the third lick. Try playing the fourth lick over and over, gradually increasing your speed to the limit.

By Arlen Roth

Using The Pick And Fingers Together

Guitar Player, January 1984.

I've been recommending the combined use of pick and fingers for a long time, especially when a delicate, country-like touch is required. Of course, this doesn't limit the effectiveness this method can have when applied to blues or rock, particularly if your nails can take it!

The advantages of using pick and fingers together are many. First, proper right-hand damping becomes almost second nature because whatever type of lick is being played, the pick and fingers are either in the process of playing the strings or resting on them. The damping will occur more naturally than, say, a situation in which only a flatpick is used, necessitating the use of the heel of your hand to cut off the notes.

Another great advantage to this technique is that rather than *dragging* across a chord with a pick, you can now *grab* three notes simultaneously, creating a much more accurate, almost piano-like attack. You then have the added option of stopping the very same notes with the same pick and fingers.

Example 24 illustrates the kind of partial chord forms that can be grabbed with the pick and two fingers. Perhaps this technique's major benefit lies in its ability to create rather complex picking patterns that can be translated into numerous positions, which could barely be executed with a flatpick alone.

Example 24.

In the banjo-like exercise in Example 25 we learn to use the pick for the hammer-on on the *D* string and the open *G*, while the in-between "drone" notes on the *B* and *E* strings are played consistently with the middle and ring fingers, respectively. You can also try breaking out of this pattern by going into a syncopated three-string run, as illustrated in Example 26.

Example 25.

Example 26.

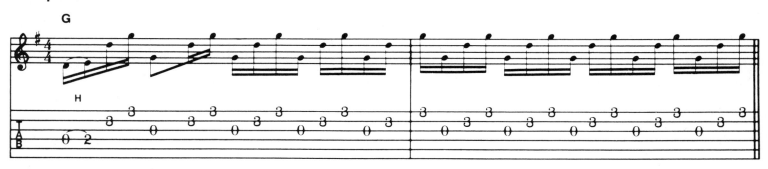

Please remember, it'll take some time for you to develop the proper independence between pick and fingers, so don't be too discouraged at first. The sole purpose of these exercises is to help you in developing this style. Keep practicing hard, and try to incorporate these new ideas into your own playing; you just might surprise yourself!

By Arlen Roth

Chapter 4:
Lead And Solo Guitar

Soloing Form

Guitar Player, May 1988.

The young guitarist Jonathan B. Goode is at his first audition, sweaty palms and all. The singer has just finished destroying the second chorus of the tune they're running down, and all eyes in the room turn to our hero for his solo. In the first two beats of the first bar, John decides to use the killer two-hand tapping arpeggio lick he'd been practicing all week. However, he's nervous, and it's new and tough, and he fluffs it. In the next two beats of bar one, he decides to redeem himself and play his trusty standby super speedball descending blues scale run, and he whips it off with the alacrity that adrenalin can provide—maybe a little too much, though, because he ends up a little ahead of the first downbeat of bar two. No problem! He just goes for the whammy bar and does what every righteous modern dude does in times of trouble: When in doubt, dump. This gives him a spectacular *sound effect* (as opposed to a musical melodic or harmonic statement) and buys him a little time to think.

On the final beat of bar two, he plays a Steve Vai lick he copped from the *Crossroads* movie guitar battle, and in bar three he plays a T-Bone Walker riff because he knows he'll score big points for showing off a knowledge of authentic roots. Uh-oh: Nine bars to go, and he's drawing a blank! So he noodles around aimlessly on the blues pentatonic (there's not too many of those weird notes to worry about there), takes another shot at the two-hander (this time around, he nails it clean, and so, buoyed by newfound confidence, repeats it ten times), runs the old faithful blues scale up the neck in thirty-second-notes and caps it off with a series of high, screaming bends up around 1,200 Hz and at about 120 decibels.

Does this story sound familiar? All you poor guys who work in music stores, isn't this the same solo you've all heard ten-million times from those young aspiring rock stars trying out new mega-gear? Let's try to be honest with each other and ourselves: When we "ad lib," just how much of what we're actually doing are we consciously aware of, and how much is truly and purely extemporaneous? How much is sincerely a personal artistic statement and how much is vapid bull shine?

There's no denying that we are assembling and exploiting pieces of our previous knowledge and experience. The art of music-making is really a constant state of fusion between what we know, what we feel, and how we can (physically and technically) express this. Improvisation is *supposed* to be short of on-the-spot composition, and in an age where we are being increasingly rigidly structured by both our technology and the programming formats of radio and record companies, we must be making an equally conscious, concerted effort to tie our feelings, personality, and our heart and soul to those moments when we are given the chance to shine our light.

How can you marry the wild, uncontrolled aesthetic passions of your soul to something as mundane and archaic as form? Well, if you are of a mind that your inner spirit should be allowed to run free, without rules or inhibiting structure, then I guess you won't find any need for my attempts at edification. The danger you face, however, in a free-form world of improvisation is that, for all intents and purposes, your work can take on an appearance of being makeshift and haphazard, even completely random, to the uninitiated and the traditionalist alike. Frankly, these qualities would not seem to have much intrinsic value, and this attitude does not lend itself to big ground support.

On the other hand, if we can accept as a basic premise that a great deal of our art is enhanced by the discipline of form, then we have added a useful ally to our cause of communicating our thoughts and feelings. As a cartoonist, a writer of prose and music lyrics, and as a guitarist, I think that form is an absolute basic necessity. You need to be so familiar with it that it seems totally natural. Indeed, you should get to the point where you are exploiting it without being conscious of it. Then it makes some real artistic sense when you say you feel the need to travel beyond its confines.

There are plenty of standard musical forms (get out your music dictionaries): strophic song, simple binary, ternary, rondo, sonata (compound binary), sonata-rondo, air with variations. Hey, even if you compose aleatoric music, opting out of historically structured

Previous page: K.K. Downing and Glen Tipton of Judas Priest.

forms has *still* slotted you into a category! (In the words of Rush's Neil Peart, "If you choose not to decide, you still have made a choice.")

But what is basic solo from? The most basic definition that would suit my purposes here is that it's just a predetermined idea in your head of structure, an overall concept, or even just a sense of purpose. The following is a compilation of quotes from many guitarists on the topic of soloing. With all due respect to the artists involved, I'd like to pirate a group of statements to build (and support) this personal theory on form:

"Before I even pick up a guitar, I'll think."

—Elliott Easton

This is an excellent start. Some guys don't even bother to think until they're actually *finished* playing, and *then* what they're thinking about is the lady in the micro-mini at the bar. Example 1a shows two contrasting phrases: Both have the same melody, but the second phrase has been well thought-out and planned. Notice fingerings, positions, use of open strings, phrasing, smoothness, and the logic of the picking pattern.

Example 1a.

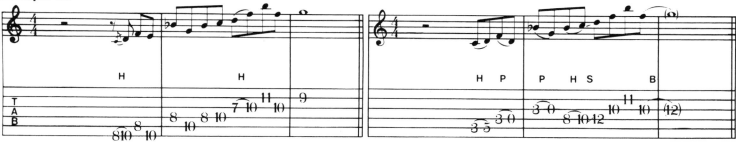

"A solo should do something. It should have some aim, take the tune somewere."

—Jeff Beck

No solo is an island. It draws life from the song around it, and should pay the favor back with interest. Example 1b shows a little melodic riff. See how Example 1c exploits the riff, in the process providing another facet to the solo, and more important, to the song as a whole.

Example 1b.   **Example 1c.**

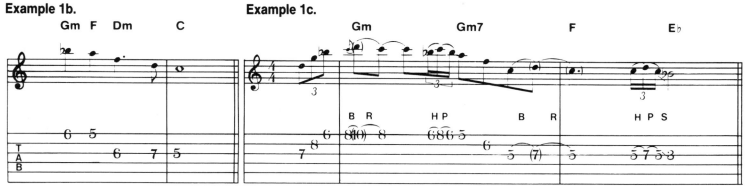

"There are four things about solo construction: the entrance, tone, building the solo, and how it's going to end. Keith Moon, who was the drummer for the Who, used to say, 'Remember, mate, they remember your entrance and your exit. Everything else in the middle don't mean a goddamn thing.' Try to make it so the end of the solo will help the next section along."

—Leslie West

Textbook performance form! When the Mountain man speaks, all cellar dwellers and garage-band blowhards should listen. Example 1c takes his advice about exiting: The vocal was coming back in on a G, so by adding a lower third harmony, I gave some extra support to his entry.

"If you blow your cookies in the first bar, you have nowhere to go."

—Tommy Bolin

Pacing, like taste, is a sign of maturity and wisdom in your playing. Some guys seem to play way beyond their years, and some cats, like Tommy or Jimi Hendrix or Charlie Christian, never even got the benefit of a lot of them. Part of their legacy is their example of exercising tasteful pacing as classic form, showing predeliberation and a firm sense of purpose in their playing.

> "Don't go in business for yourself until you know what the composer had in mind . . . The [good players] are giving you a message, and the message is not how many notes they are playing; it's the feeling they get."
>
> —*Herb Ellis*

What's the attitude of a song? What is the emotion? How well are you capturing it and interpreting it?

> "A solo should be a statement, like a good novel. It should start someplace, grab your interest, work up to a climax, and then go down and lead into . . . whatever comes next. And it should follow a theme."
>
> —*Pat Travers*

Solos that are a constant stream of climaxes end up having no climax at all. A (slightly tongue-in-cheek) line-graph illustration of a "standard" song concept based on the Barry Manilow ballad formula arrangement, containing such a solo form, might look something like Example 2.

Example 2.

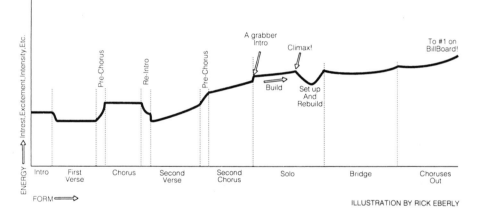

ILLUSTRATION BY RICK EBERLY

> "It's like trying to describe something to someone; it's a conversation where you say something in a certain way."
>
> —*B.B. King*

And we all know what a succinctly eloquent lady Lucille is.

I particularly like the analogies to speech, or writing stories. The most basic writing structure is the essay, and I think it behooves us to take a look at that particular form. Notice how it bears a remarkable resemblance to West's and Travers' outlines:

1. Introduction
2. Body (argument)
3. Conclusion

An introduction should have a strong lead, or hook, to get the reader (listener) interested, and should clearly state the thesis, the main proposition, theme, or argument of the piece. The main body of the essay contains a convincing elaboration, illustration, and defense of the thesis. And the textbook definition of a proper conclusion should have three things: a restatement of the main thesis, a summation of the points raised in the main body, and your closing remark (having the last word in an argument, if you will, and making it a real zinger).

My use of essay form is only an illustrative example. You may personally and quite rightly find it inappropriate, in that you can easily envision one solo constructed along the lines of, say, climbing Led Zeppelin's "Stairway To Heaven," and another song's solo being nothing more than a driving one-note wonder. (Remember Crazy Horse's "Cinnamon Girl"? Now, it's not what I would have chosen to do, but it leaves an undeniably effective impression.) All I am suggesting is that concept breeds form, and some forms are more universal than others. In some contexts, form can simply be pure emotion: "I get the blues, and I just let go in the middle of it," said Muddy Waters.

We've looked at form as a basic ingredient in building a good solo. Form is just a solid, personal concept of structure, a sort of general outline. Once you get past the physically technical point of being able to pick out the notes and get from one to the next, how do you express your personality through them? Example 3 shows the same melodic riff played from four different stylistic sensibilities, which gives us four different stories. This illustrates the technical interpretations inherent in any given musical statement. What it doesn't show are the personal, *emotional* interpretations that are possible: Dynamics, phrasing, and stylistic variations can occur on, between, or inside any given note in any of the four examples (not to mention the amount of vibrato you employ, or where you're moving the picking position around on the string, or how slowly or quickly you reach your destination on bends or slurs, etc.).

Example 3.

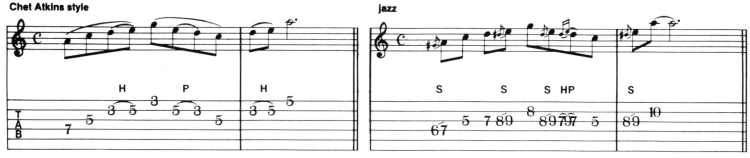

"To truly improvise requires you not to know anything, in a sense. In this state of mind you see everything before you, every possibility. All avenues suddenly open to you."

—*John McLaughlin*

"You know, you can tell when someone makes a speech from his heart; it's just spontaneous."

—*Carlos Santana*

You sense bad actors or politicians because the speeches that come out of their mouths are unnatural and rehearsed-sounding. But a truly great acting job isn't really acting at all, because the actor has become the character, and there is a symbiotic flow between the role and the person playing it. And therein lies their true art.

How can I teach you to get in touch with yourself? That's something we've all got to do on our own. Still, there are some concepts that can get you away from the guitaristic technical traps and move you towards the discovery of your "inner voice."

"Make your solo as vocally oriented as possible, just as if someone were singing it, so the sound grows more human and natural."

—*Ronnie Montrose*

Historically, by nature, the sound of acoustic guitars was front-end loaded with percussive attack and a relatively swift decay with no sustain to speak of (see Example 4). Blues players such as Tampa Red and Robert Johnson changed all that by popularizing slide guitar, which could give the guitar the sliding, bending, and the legato effects of a human voice (Example 5). In the '30s, George Barnes and Eddie Durham pioneered the use of the electric guitar in jazz. By the late '30s, clarinetist Benny Goodman's guitarist Charlie Christian popularized the instrument, playing amplified guitar lines that were heavily inspired by the tenor sax work of Lester Young (refer to Example 6). The phrasing and concepts of horn players are very vocally oriented, as well, since they also run on lung power.

Example 4.   **Example 5.**

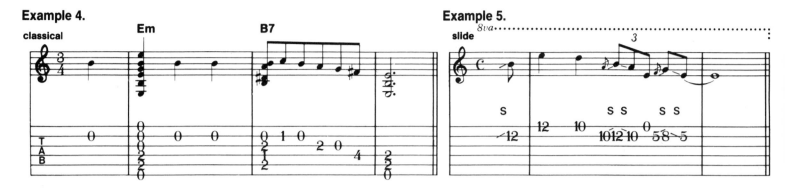

Example 6.

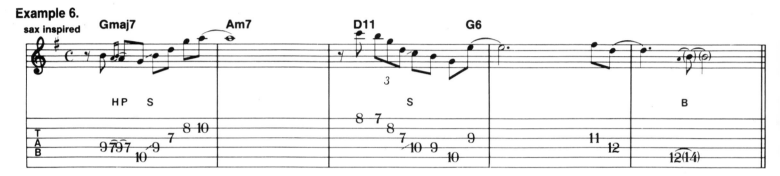

In the late '50s James Burton put slinky banjo strings on his guitar to ease his string-bending leads on Ricky Nelson's "Believe What You Say." Now guitarists could imitate the sliding and bending of a voice or another instrument quite easily (Example 7).

"If you want extreme guitar playing, you should listen to Paganini. His way of playing the violin was kind of the way I wanted to play guitar."

—*Yngwie Malmsteen*

Check out Example 8 for an arpeggio in the Yngwie style of Paganini. Volume, distortion, and sustain (not to mention whammy bars) have all increased the range of a guitar's interpretive and expressive solo potential. We can see how the fusion of such diverse elements as creative personality and technical advance can lead to a higher ground, and so the potential of MIDI synthesis is another exciting option for the brave artistic soul. Yet it will always come back to this: It won't amount to a hill of beans unless it

Example 7.   **Example 8.**

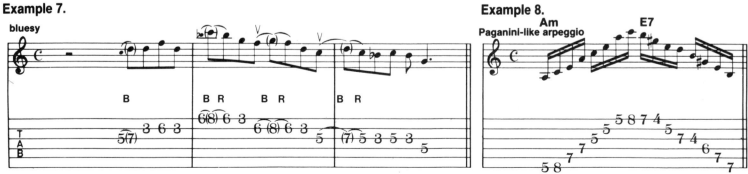

is your voice, your *personality* in the solo. How do you feel, what do you think, what do you know? For all of the infinite possibilities that lie outside the physical and technical borders that exist, there is an equally infinite potential that dwells inside each and every artist.

By Rik Emmett

Warming Up

Guitar Player, **September, October 1987.**

One of the many positive things that can come from being thrust into the role of teacher is that your students inevitably present a challenge, forcing you to analyze things you've taken for granted or grown unconscious of. If you're open to it, this role reversal can bring about rediscovery and an opportunity to acquaint yourself with the most up-to-date modifications and new points of view.

Case in point: At a guest lecture/seminar at Toronto's Humber College, a student asked me to show him some warm-up exercises. I didn't know what to tell him. I had never consciously analyzed what the heck I was doing, or had been forced to explain why. I had always just fiddled around until I felt ready.

So now I intend to consciously apply myself to one of these questions and present what I consider to be a "greatest hits" package of essential, basic warm-ups (minus the usual unconscious noodling, the impromptu cover versions of "Wipe Out" or "Secret Agent Man," and the degeneration into comic parody that has become a personal dressing-room hallmark).

Before we get into this, let's just remember the simple things that one is trying to accomplish with a warm-up:

Physical and mental preparation

Relaxation

Confidence for the task at hand

First I usually run a few scales, starting very slowly and methodically, and then increasing the tempo and adding dynamics. I frequently employ some form of the scales in Example 9. I try to mix them up a little, from a picking point of view, warming up with hammer-ons and pull-offs for the left hand (Example 10), and cross-string picking for the

Example 9.

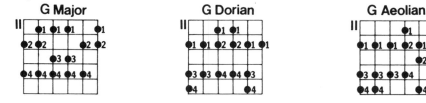

Example 10.

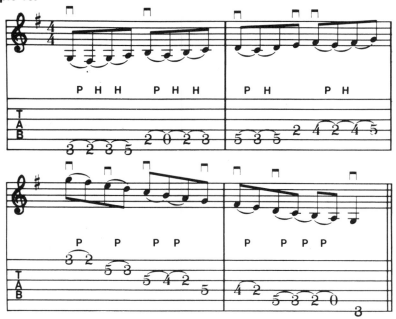

right (Example 11). This tends to jump-start the coordination between both hands.

Then I begin to concentrate on my meter and timing, getting a feel for finding the pocket. I try some scalar-type licks and runs (Example 12), and then probably play something in triplets (Example 13). These help me get comfortable with shifting and changing positions. At this point I might throw in a few Steve Cropper or Albert King licks and start jamming a 12-bar blues with myself, using straight lead and some jazz chord-melodies.

Example 11.

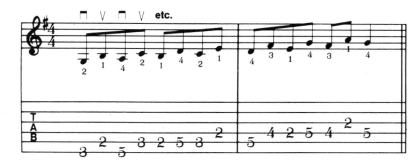

Example 12.

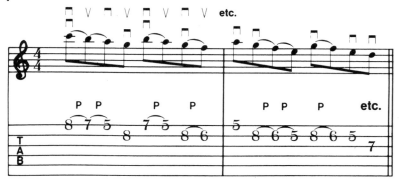

Example 13.

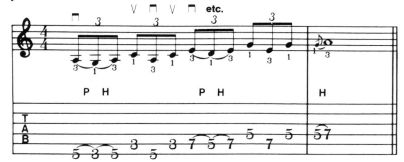

Once I feel good and relaxed, I tackle the more intense part of the warm-up. When the motor is idling fairly smoothly, I usually prepare my hands by practicing a few of the strenuous virtuoso-style licks I'll have to play on the gig (Examples 14 and 15). Then I get

Example 14.

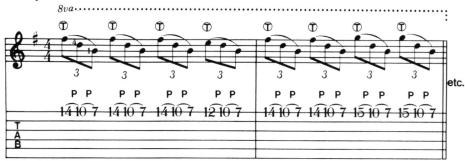

Example 15.

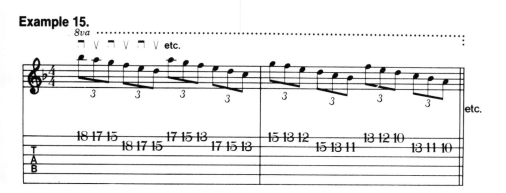

Example 16.

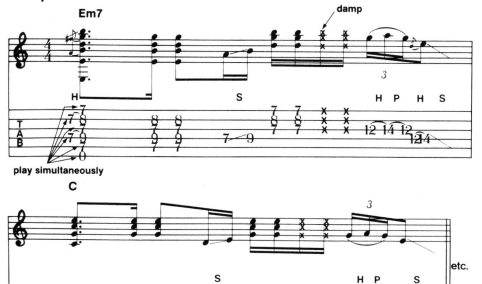

play simultaneously

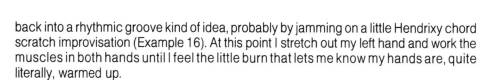

back into a rhythmic groove kind of idea, probably by jamming on a little Hendrixy chord scratch improvisation (Example 16). At this point I stretch out my left hand and work the muscles in both hands until I feel the little burn that lets me know my hands are, quite literally, warmed up.

By Rik Emmett

Pivoting Exercises For Both Hands

Guitar Player, July 1987.

You may know a "pivot" as being in conjunction with the kind of B.B. King-like vibrato, where the left hand pivots off the side of the neck to produce the proper movement needed for the vibrato. In the case of this discussion, however, the pivot is actually a musical situation in which one note is held down while the others move. This is an excellent power and accuracy builder for your right-hand picking, because it forces you to work very quickly within relatively tight spaces and teaches you economy of motion. It's important to maintain an up-and-down picking motion for these pieces, and to start them relatively slowly and build up speed as you go along. The idea is to play them fast. You'll find that for many of you, the faster you play this style, the easier it is to execute. The technique is hard to demonstrate slowly, since I only use it when playing rapidly.

Be sure to let the pick "dance" over the strings for these, since it has to jump strings many times. This requires a very relaxed and loose wrist, but at the same time, great accuracy. I'm quite sure that once you've worked these into your style, the benefits will be quite apparent.

This first group of exercises in Example 17 deals with a pivot off of the *B* string, while the moving notes are on the high *E*. You could experiment with using a barre with the 1st finger, but I wouldn't recommend that you waste a lot of energy by maintaining it throughout the entire lick.

Example 17.

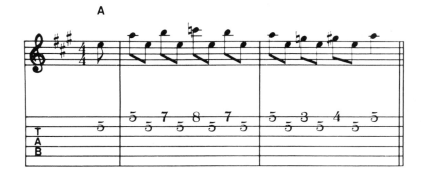

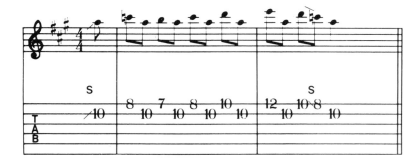

The bunch of licks in Example 18 involves a jump from the *G* string to the high *E* string, and tests your accuracy a bit more than the previous group. Start the *G*-string notes with a downstroke, while using an upstroke for the notes on the high *E* string.

This final group of exercises (Example 19) mixes things up a bit, in that they pivot between the *G* and *E* strings while throwing in an occasional *B* string note, as well. I

Example 18.

Example 19.

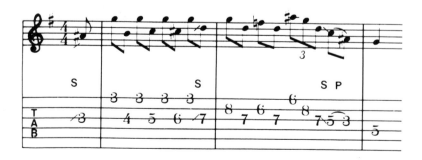

encourage you to use these to find some of your own pivot licks, for the possibilities are truly infinite. You'll see that once the technique is under your control, the ideas will really start to flow. So practice and practice, but have fun while you're doing it. And most of all keep those ears and fingers open to new ideas!

By Arlen Roth

Rock Licks And Tricks

Guitar Player, December 1983.

For as long as I've been playing, I've periodically heard people complain that the guitar isn't laid out logically. It isn't as easy to see the notes as on the piano, and that makes it inaccessible and hard to play harmonically—or so they say. To counter those arguments, I've found that the guitar has a lot of built-in advantages over, say, a piano, or any other instrument that is laid out chromatically. What the guitar can be is a *trickster* instrument. It happens to be tuned very closely to an *Em* (E minor) chord, and therefore we're going to talk about some of the tricks that you can do based on the key of *E* minor. These can be used in songs (and I've used them in *many* songs), in solo work or rhythm work, or just as exercises.

Examples 20, 21, and 22, in this article are derived from the *E* Dorian mode. Since they're based on an *E* minor sound, they work great in either an *E* minor or *G* major context (*E* minor is the relative minor of *G* major). So if you're in either key, these ideas can come in handy.

Our first example uses a moving tenth interval (the notes on the fifth and second strings) combined with open strings. Note how the open sixth string helps retain the *E* tonality. Although you can use just your right-hand finger to pluck the strings, I prefer to use my fingers and a pick: Pluck the high *E* string with your pinky, the *B* with your ring finger, the *G* with your middle finger, and the low *E* and *A* strings with your pick, which should be held with the thumb and index finger (see Example 20).

Example 20.

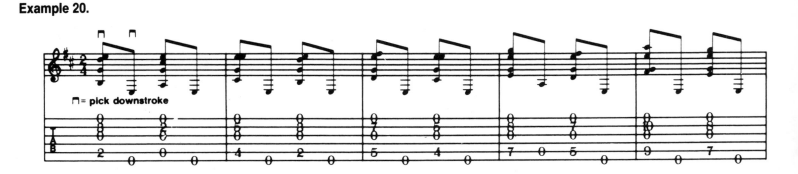

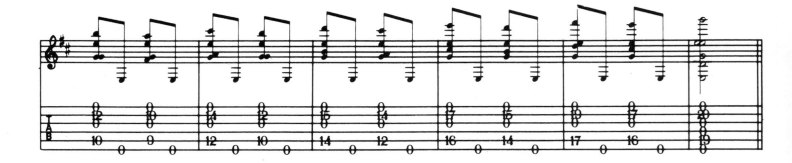

Let's go on to a little bit trickier-sounding lick. This one can be used in soloing, and makes a good exercise. It's especially helpful because it incorporates some pull-offs. Most of us are used to playing pull-offs on a single string, so one of the things that I like about this exercise is that it uses both the *B* and the *E* strings, plus there's some double picking and plucking action. With your right hand, pluck the *E* string with the middle finger and strike the *B* string with the pick (which is held by the thumb and index finger).

This next exercise (Example 21) provides very good practice for your right hand as well as your left hand. It's also good for developing your eye-hand coordination. Like the first example, it can be worked into a lot of songs and solo passages. Played faster, it gives a cascading effect. Fast or slow, it's very useful.

When you encounter an *Em* or *G* chord, these things will sound good as embellishments. Think of them as tricks. They're specifically from the guitar and *for* the guitar. So whenever anyone gives you the argument about the guitar being poorly laid out, you have these kinds of things to pull from your bag—to show them that they can be wrong sometimes. Facility with these will enable you to be a flashier player.

Example 21.

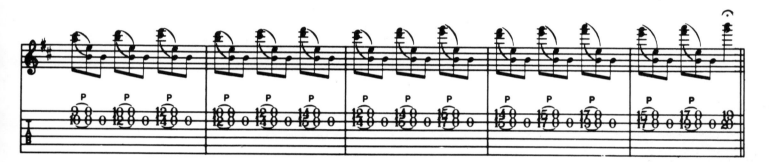

The next trick (Example 22) I'll demonstrate sounds a little like banjo picking. You could pluck it with your fingers, but we'll approach it with a pick, because the picking action is a good workout for your hand. This technique is pretty simple, and again it's a Dorian minor trick that's especially tailored to your instrument. (Note that your guitar must have at least 21 frets for the exercise.)

Example 22.

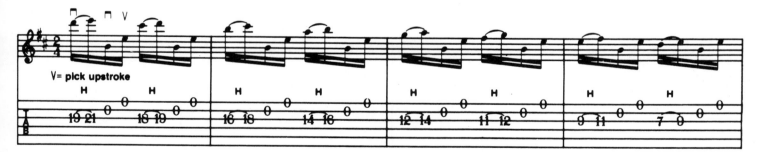

Okay! Our final example (see Example 23) is something that I don't think many people try on a guitar, and a lot of guitarists would find it hard to figure out just by listening. Many years ago, a friend showed me exactly how to do this, a series of licks that you've heard Ray Charles do a lot in his piano playing (and certainly a lot of other pianists do it, too). But there aren't many guitarists who do it. It's the only example of all four we've explored that isn't in *E* minor. You can use it in any key, but here it's in *A*.

Example 23.

We'll perform double-stops by plucking the high *E* string with the middle finger, the *B* or *G* string with the pick—held by the middle finger—for the single notes, and pick either down or up, according to the instructions in the music. There's a little ritard (*ritardando*, or slowing down) at the end and some glissandos, so it's good for your picking technique and your sensitivity. There are a lot of different techniques to put to use here. Great! This ending can be used throughout songs or solos, or as the finale of a tune.

All of the techniques in this lesson can be elaborated upon in many different ways. They're great when combined, and are a good basis for further experimentation.

By Rick Derringer

Hot Lead Licks

Guitar Player, **August 1986.**

Constant Bass Licks

One of the great ways to build tension and intensity as a lead *or* rhythm player is the technique of juxtaposing a constant bass pattern against some licks or fills. Both right-hand techniques—either all flatpicking or the pick-and-fingers approach—work equally well, though the latter obviously allows you to hit every bass note, while the former forces you to sacrifice some of the bass notes when you need to pick the lead lines. The end result is similar, and the truly experienced flatpicker can execute these kinds of licks very well. It should be pointed out that, while this style is often associated with rhythm playing, it also applies to lead and can be put to good use in solos.

Example 24 is reminiscent of the playing of Pete Townshend, who so effectively uses the constant bass pattern over chords. This kind of piece should be played with all downstrokes, which add to the aggressive quality. Make sure to let the picking hand leave the bass notes just enough to catch the chords on the beat.

It's also a pleasure to be able to catch certain higher, closed postions off this kind of lick. Example 25 is reminiscent of gospel or rockabilly; note how you can also use techniques such as hammer-ons in these licks with great results.

Perhaps the truest test of your accuracy within this style is when you can manage the constant bass while picking out single notes with the flatpick, as in Example 26. The addition of hammer-ons and pull-offs enable the left hand to play more notes, while the right hand can get back to the work of keeping the bass notes going. This homogenizing of the two parts is essential to creating a smooth technique, expecially if you're flatpicking and want to approximate a fingerpicked-like effect.

Example 24.

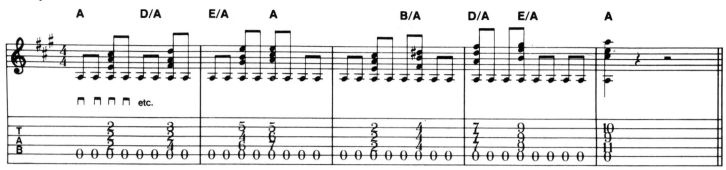

Example 25.

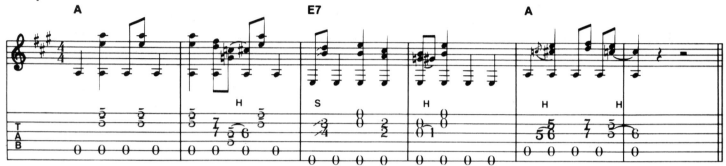

Example 26.

Big Stretches

There are a lot of us who use rather conventional positions for lead guitar and rely on the very popular and somewhat overplayed technique of right-hand tapping to get notes that are off in the stratosphere. That's okay, and in many cases it's the only way of getting to these notes. There are, however, a lot of more traditional "stretch" positions I like to use in blues and rock playing that are of a similar nature to the now-familiar right-hand "taps-on."

Many of these positions came as a result of experimenting within the traditional blues "box" scales, and the need to branch out a bit within them. Since I'm an unchangeable three-fingered player, my left-hand pinky is really too weak to play a lot of these—so I've actually been making four-, five-, and six-fret stretches with my 3rd finger all this time! I do this by simply letting my finger creep up the side of the fretboard and catch the given note almost from underneath it. You can try this method, too, but I'm sure that most of you would prefer to use your pinky for these licks. It's important that you build up your pinky's strength, and these exercises can be great, particularly in the more demanding performing situations, where acrobatics and flash also count.

The pattern in Example 27 is a series of left-hand stretches combined with rapid pull-offs. Note the changing of the chords implied by the licks. These all employ a partial index-finger barre over the top two strings, and again, you may try either the 3rd finger or the pinky to make the long stretch.

We can now use the same index-finger barre on the high *E* and *B* strings, but the stretch pull-offs can occur on the *B* instead of the *E*. In Example 28 the pattern also includes a nice two-note hammer-on going up on the *B* string.

Once we've gotten used to playing these stretches in relatively stationary positions, it's another whole challenge to try moving them up the fingerboard, especially while not breaking stride or losing a beat. This simply improves with practice, as the patterns and positions become well-established in your mind's eye before they are played. Take special note that Example 29's positions, while played one right after the other, are not exactly the same, and they involve subtle changes in positioning on your part.

Example 27.

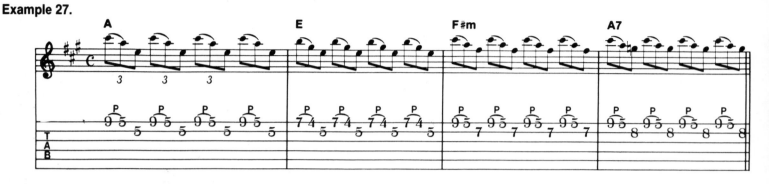

Example 28.

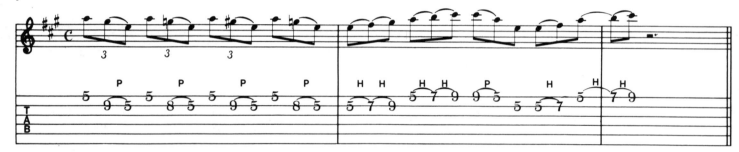

Example 29.

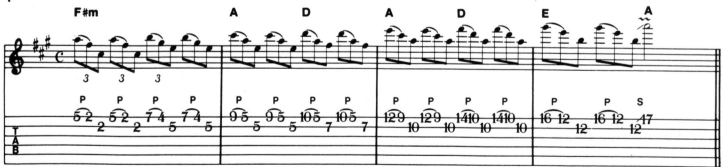

Southern Rock Harmonies For One

The sound of so-called "Southern Rock" has long been associated with double-guitar harmony parts. This was pioneered and best exemplified by Duane Allman and Dickey Betts of the original Allman Brothers Band. It then went on to become part of the sound of countless other Southern rockers, such as the Marshall Tucker Band, Lynyrd Skynyrd, and more recently in the country rock of Charlie Daniels, Alabama, and Hank Williams, Jr. This double-guitar sound eventually reached places such as New York and L.A., as you can hear in Elliot Randall's solo on Steely Dan's "Reeling In The Years" [*Steely Dan—Greatest Hits*, MCA, 2-6008] and on the guitar break in just about any lush big-production-type ballad of the '70s.

I have always been intrigued with the prospect and challenge of creating these kinds of parts with one guitar. Generally speaking, many of the well-known harmony solos began freely, like any other solo, then eventually built into a repeating pattern before finally becoming harmonized as the second part entered. Note that this technique can be used to great effect for unison playing and octaves, as well as harmonies.

In the solo in Example 30, I've re-created a typical way in which one of these harmony solos can be developed. The only difference is that you're actually playing the two parts by yourself. This requires some very accurate fingering in tight spaces, and it can get a little crowded. So be careful, and take it slow at first—especially when it comes to hammer-ons and pull-offs.

Example 30.

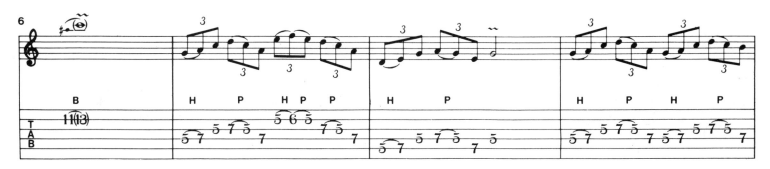

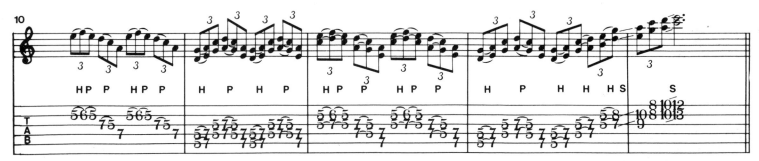

Open-Position "Roll" Licks

As an interesting variation on the same old shuffles and open-position licks one is called on to play as a guitarist, I've come up with some open-position "roll" licks. I call them this because they are best played with a pick-and-fingers approach, utilizing a hammer-on and barre-position combination that lends itself to the "roll" sound. For those familiar with my recordings, this style is best exemplified on my song "Restless Age," from the *Hot Pickups* LP [Rounder, 3044].

For the pick-and-fingers approach, use the flatpick and both the middle and ring fingers for the following exercises. The pick is involved only on the lowest string of each lick, and then the other fingers following the remaining strings in natural order. It's important when assuming the "ready" position for these licks that the pick and fingers be already positioned on the strings themselves. This not only helps you achieve the roll sound properly, it enables you to damp the strings until they are needed. This way, we can move this three-stringed grouping conveniently from one chord to another in a sort of "block" formation.

Left-hand partial barres are necessary and helpful, since you can place many hammer-ons and pull-offs directly over them; just be sure to press them down firmly enough to make them sustain well. If you can put all of these techniques together successfully into one package, you should be able to tackle this style with ease. If not, then one little hitch in the system could make things difficult for you. In any event, let's try

Example 31 in the open position of *E*. Have your pick and fingers in the ready position before you start, and be sure to play all of the hammers and pulls as indicated.

In Example 32 we have variations on the standard roll pattern. In this case, we are using pull-offs and the open *D* string to change things around. My favorite open position for roll licks is *A*. Here we can literally duplicate what we were doing for *E*, moved up one string to the *A, D,* and *G* strings. Example 33 shows the standard position and the newer variations all rolled into one.

The position for *D* (Example 34) doesn't contain a partial barre, but it is no more difficult to execute than the *E* or *A* positions. The only real trick lies in using the 2nd finger as part of the initial hammer-on on the *D* string, just before it crosses over to be used on the *B* string.

Finally, in Example 35 we have the same type of roll for open *G*, played on the high three strings. Since a more radical shift in position is required, we'll use a *slide* with our 2nd finger on the *G* string to simulate what the hammer-ons were doing in the previous examples. Try to incorporate these exercises into your own ideas.

By Arlen Roth

Example 31.

Example 32.

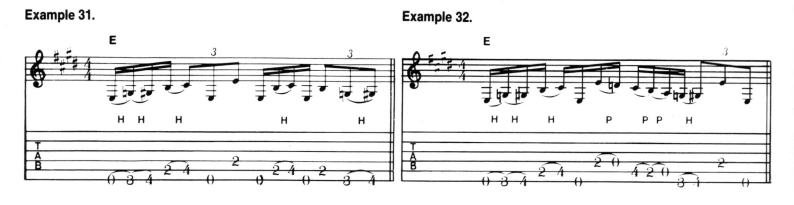

Example 33.

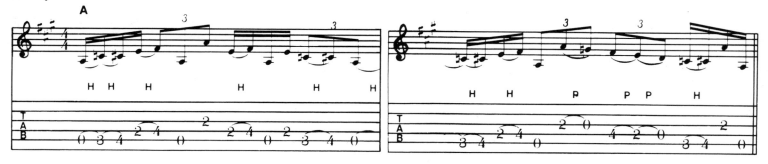

Example 34.

Example 35.

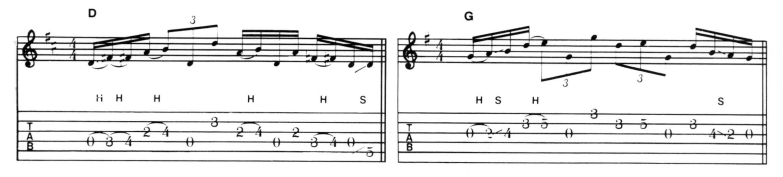

Speed

With John Duarte and Frank Gambale

Chops are something most guitarists want, but too few know how to attain efficiently. In this section we'll take an in-depth look at speed development for pickstyle and fingerstyle technique. While scale facility is fundamental to music and dazzling when executed on the guitar, it's also one of the instrument's most elusive skills—but not impossible to cultivate. With the help of the teaching and performing talents of masters John Duarte and Frank Gambale, you'll gain rare insight into fine-tuning your ability to play fast.

In some respects, there are as many approaches to technique as there are guitarists. For instance, some pickstyle players rest their right wrist on the bridge, while others support the hand in one way or another with the right-hand pinky. Likewise, for fast scale passages many fingerstylists bring their right hand closer to the soundboard, while others retain their normal hand position. (In addition, when executing scales, fingerstyle players usually stabilize the right hand by either keeping the thumb on the sixth string or supported against some of the strings.) For the most part, however, fast players agree on a number of aspects of scale speed development, including slow repetition, daily practice, the use of a metronome, and working systematically.

This discussion on speed is geared toward the guitarist with some knowledge of left-hand scale fingerings. (Many of the exercises in the following articles can be used by pickstyle *and* fingerstyle players.)

High-speed playing involves precise coordination of the right and left hands. While novices need to focus on both equally, more advanced players often have one that is more developed than the other. To see if you fit into the latter category, try the following experiment: Play Example 36 (which uses only hammer-ons) as fast and evenly as possible: Now attempt to articulate each note—with either a pick or your fingers—at the same tempo. If your right hand can't keep up with your left, then it needs special attention (one of the trickier aspects of right-hand scale technique involves crossing from one string to the next).

Andres Segovia recommended, "Build a technique to cover all difficulties, slowly with efficiency. The angels of Jacob came up and down the ladder step by step, although they had wings."

What Speed Is And How To Use It

The one question I get asked more often than any other is: "How can I improve my speed?" It sometimes seems as if we're in an age that is *obsessed* by speed and that it's all-important, while those who don't have it are apt to tell you that it isn't really essential and that musicality is foremost. In the final analysis, musicality and expression are what sorts the sheep from the goats. Ultrasonic speed coupled with substandard musicality reduces a player to the level of a skilled acrobat or juggler—and there are more than a few of those around! However, playing fast is an important part of the overall musical picture. Before we take a look at how you acquire speed, let's put things in perspective.

Variety and contrast of all kinds are fundamentally important in any art; without them, all you have is cultured monotony. Speed is one kind of variety—animation. Without it you get monotony of pace. Throughout the course of an evening, a good player offers contrasts of speed, but only if he or she is capable of a good range of velocity. Anyone can play slowly (though not necessarily well, since slow playing has its own special problems), but it's your highest speed that sets the limit to your ability to provide contrast. This doesn't mean that you're wasting your time if you're not the fastest gun in town, but it does mean that you need a reasonable upper limit if you aren't going to ultimately bore the pants off your audience.

Another virtue of speed is that it gives you a *safety factor*. Suppose that your ceiling is sixteenth-notes played at ♩=100 (playing four sixteenth-notes at ♩=100 produces 400 of them per minute). If this common tempo represents your upper limit, you'll be near the edge more often than you care to be—where you might pull it off, but you just might

Guitar Player, September 1987.

Example 36.

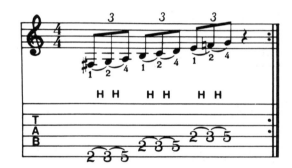

fail, if only because you're anxious about it. However, if you can handle sixteenths at $\downarrow =$ 120, ones based on $\downarrow = 100$ are going to be easier and safer (and if you can reach 150, you'll be well within your capacity, so no sweat). Just because you can play fast doesn't necessarily mean that you'll never need to reach your top speed, but the higher it is, the more comfortable you'll be at lower ones. Think of it this way: Would you feel safe getting into an elevator loaded to its stated capacity? You might, but only it it has been tested well beyond the stated limit. A Jaguar or a Porsche does have a use in a country where you can't legally drive faster than 55 mph. For instance, with a car that can do twice the legal speed limit, you have an ample reserve of power and acceleration to get you out of trouble. And at 55, your Porsche or Jaguar isn't working hard and wearing out fast. A good reserve of speed means that you can play with more relaxation, knowing that you aren't being uncomfortably stretched.

Remember that there's nothing wrong or sinful about being able to play fast! Comparatively few things are bad in themselves, but even fewer are the ones than cannot be put to bad use. Guns are not bad things by definition, but they are put to many bad uses—by bad people! Any good artist is entitled to play his or her strong suit; if you've got speed, display it, but only as one facet of your ability and as a means of getting maximum variety in your performances. It is only when speed is just about all you have to offer that it becomes empty. (A corollary to this line of thought is that you should never play anything in a concert that is dangerously near your limit, keeping in mind that a piece is as difficult as its hardest measure. It's better to stay slow and get things right; there is no prize for brave failure.)

Nuts And Bolts

So much for healthy (and unhealthy) attitudes toward speed. What about the nuts and bolts of the matter? Messages are transmitted through your body at the same high rate as they are through everyone else's, so playing fast ultimately depends upon how efficiently those signals are translated into actions. Your brain tells your body to do something just as fast as everyone else's—but how fast do you react to the message? In your mind you might be able to leave John McLaughlin or Pepe Romero in your exhaust smoke, but not with your fingers! I believe that we all have our own built-in limit, printed into our systems like the color of our hair or the shape of our face, although conditioning may determine how far away from it we are at a particular time. There are slow people and fast people—slow responders and quick ones. If I were to unknowingly walk into the path of a moving car, I'd rather the driver were someone who could run scales at 800 notes-per-minute instead of someone who had trouble at half that speed!

If most of us are never going to be up with the front-runners because our motor responses have lower upper limits, the best we can do is to work to reach our own maximum. Don't be too upset when you find your limit to be lower than someone else's; worrying about it is liable to make matters worse.

How fast is it posible to play? Is there a human limit beyond which no one can go? I believe there is. There are various ways of making rough estimates, based on the way the human body and nervous system function, but a reasonable parallel can be drawn from motion pictures. If you run a film slowly enough, the action becomes jerky and you start to see the separate frames and lose the illusion of smooth, continuous movement. That critical speed is about 21 frames-per-second—1,260 per minute. Now if separate messages in the form of pictures become blurred into quasi-continuity at a certain rate of presentation, it only follows that beyond a given speed, it's impossible to differentiate separate notes of a scale or arpeggio. I have not witnessed the experiment, but it seems probable that if a chromatic scale, say, were played at a speed above 1,300 notes-per-minute (as it easily could be with a digital sequencer), it would be heard as a glissando. The brain might well be unable to register each note separately at that speed, resulting in the aural equivalent of a motion picture. In fact, the fastest players I have ever heard can reach only approximately 1,000 notes per minute (sixteenth-notes played a $\downarrow = 250$), and then only in well-rehearsed scales or right-hand arpeggiations that involve no right-or left-hand coordination problem. I have yet to hear an instrumentalist reach 1,200 notes-per-minute! Allowing for the inefficiency of our bodies, 1,000 notes per minute seems a reasonable "ceiling."

How can you reach your maximum? To be able to run, you must first learn to walk properly. Fast playing begins with careful and sharply targeted slow playing; if you don't believe this, forget the whole thing—we're both wasting our time. If you can't play slowly and very precisely with optimally "engineered" mental and physical approaches, you certainly won't be able to play fast, any more than you can make your music better by buying the loudest amp on the market. You must develop the ability to "hear" and "think" every note as a real, spearate thing. A fast passage is a rapid succession of musical notes, not the product of a frantic, panic-stricken flapping of the fingers.

Beyond this simple advice—which may be difficult to accept if you're impatient—there is another layer that is often equally unwelcome, but essential. Remember, if you adhere to the following guidelines, you'll only arrive at your goal that much quicker:

1. Never begin a day's practice by trying to play fast. Always start slowly and deliberately. Athletes don't jump out of bed, throw on their gear, and go straight out of the door to try to break Olympic records; they spend a little time getting their bodies used to the fact that another day has dawned and another start has to be made.

2. Use a metronome to monitor your work. You are probably much less good at making estimates (what north-country English people call measuring "by the rack of the eye") than you think. If you don't believe this, try to judge the exact length of something just by looking at it, and then get out your ruler to see how far out you are! The same applies to all your faculties, including assessment of speed. The metronome is much better at it than you are. So why is this important? It not only tells you exactly what you're doing, but it also enables you to measure precisely the increases you make.

3. Having started the day's work, increase speed gradually. The speed of what? Whatever you start with! Most professionals and amateur players begin with scales or set patterns, which allow you to concentrate on the real business of getting your actions and timing in good shape. Set the metronome at a low rate (even a funereal one), and don't raise the speed until you can play whatever it is repeatedly and without mistakes. Again, if you can't do it slowly, you can't do it faster. When you're ready to raise the speed of the metronome, edge it up by no more than 10 percent (for instance, raise 60 to 66, or 66 to 72, etc.). When the pace begins to get hot, reduce your increases to 5 percent. Consolidate at every stage before moving up. It's easy enough to grit your teeth and set a low starting pace, but when you decide you can go a bit faster, you must be very careful of how far you go. If you are not very good at judging such things unaided, what you think is a small amount may actually be a lot. My advice is to avoid quantum leaps, instead opting for gradual transitions that don't overtax your technique. The closer you approach your maximum, the more damaging such overestimates can be, which is why you need to reduce the size of upward steps. When you reach a speed at which you can no longer get things right, stop there. Any further attempted acceleration will do damage, not good.

You may find that your maximum speed varies from one day to the next. Improvement does not take place continuously—it has ups and downs, but it should average out over a period of weeks or even months. If progress comes to a halt over a long time frame, it could be due to a couple of reasons. First, progress sometimes occurs in quantum leaps, for a variety of reasons that we may or may not understand (at the time, at least). Your technique, or any facet of it, may reach a plateau and stay there for several months, after which it mysteriously and dramatically advances. Second, you may simply have reached your own ceiling. Only time will tell.

There are always exceptional people who seem to acquire speed naturally and with little effort; they don't need to warm up but can play fluently at any time of the day or night. For the less fortunate majority of guitarists, speed must be approached slowly, gradually, systematically, and patiently along the lines I've described. One final point: You can scramble through something with your metronome set at 152, say, with some missed or dirty notes, but if you play it at 120 cleanly, it will sound faster!

Everything finally depends on your mental and physical approach; it's not enough just to be grimly determined to play fast (whatever that may be for you). In fact, such an attitude is self-destructive. Don't neglect slow practice; it gives you a firm base and allows you to check that your technique is working correctly. Any basic flaw in technique will be magnified by speed. Additionally, don't ruin your coordination by playing too fast too soon in the day, rushing your objective like an infuriated warthog. Speed up gradually and under control, so that you build a foundation of confidence.

Relax. The more tense and uptight you get, the worse it will be. Tension works against you, not for you. If you get anxious and tense—which can affect what you do even before you get to it—knowing that a fast passage is approaching, your muscles will tighten and you'll never make it! Relax and let it happen.

Finally, if after all your efforts you can't raise a satisfactory speed—and I'd say that anyone who can't handle sixteenth-note scales at $\downarrow$=112 (approximately 450 notes per minute) has a real problem—go to a good teacher. Odds are that your basic technique is at fault.

Sweep Picking

For the last 15 years I have devoted myself to what I call sweep picking—a technique that can be used in place of alternate picking (or in addition to it) to develop considerable speed. Many players use some sweep picking licks without realizing how far the approach can be taken.

The most common pickstyle method uses strict alternate strokes (down, up, down, up, etc.); however, some players opt for a less articulated effect, where a picked note is followed by hammer-ons and/or pull-offs. In sweep picking, the same pick stroke is used to play from two to six notes. Depending on the phrase, some alternate picking is employed. The economy of sweep picking enables you to play a lot of notes with minimal movement of the picking hand, making it easier to play at high velocities.

Look at Example 37, an *A* major scale fingering. Since it has three notes per string, there is a tendency to give it a triplet feel, so be sure to practice it in groups of two or four notes per beat (eighths and sixteenths, respectively). At first, only practice the ascending version of Example 37. When you're comfortable with that, work on the descending sequence; many players find ascending sweeps much more natural feeling.

When sweep picking it's important to remember the following points:

1. Keep the notes as separate as possible—almost *staccato* (short) at first, especially when crossing strings. Newcomers to sweep picking tend to run the notes together.

2. Watch your right hand and make sure that you are using a *single* movement when crossing strings, not two separate successive strokes.

3. Always practice with a metronome or a drum machine, making sure that the notes are clean and even. Be critical and honest when evaluating yourself.

4. It's harder to sweep at slower tempos, so start with medium ones (sixteenths at ♩ = 60 to 100).

Rule: Sweep picking licks require an odd number of notes per string. In Example 37 notice that there are three notes per string going up and three notes per string going down. To reverse the direction of the sweep stroke in a line, you need an even number of notes on the string where the reversal takes place. The two consectuive notes on the first string in Example 37 facilitate the change of direction.

The sweep pattern for Example 37 is very important, since practically any scale (and its inversions) can be fingered using three notes per string. This simplifies the number of patterns you need to know. It also eliminates problem spots in conventional scale patterns, where two notes per string occur in certain places. The ideal scale scheme features three notes on the *E, A, D, G,* and *B* strings, and two notes on the high *E*, which allows you to reverse the direction of the pick stroke for a descending sweep.

Example 37.

A major scale

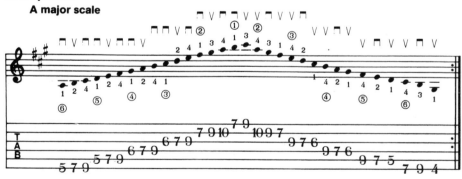

Example 38 is a sweep configuration for an *A* pentatonic (five-note scale) position; observe that the sweeps cross three strings. The odd/even rule still applies. Since there are only two notes on the sixth string, begin with an upstroke so that you can sweep onto the fifth string and set things up for the rest of the scale. The entire pattern goes: Two notes on the sixth string, three on the fifth, one on the fourth, three on the third, and one on the second. There are two notes on the first string for the direction change. The preceding example requires quite a bit of left-hand stretching; allowing your left-hand thumb and fingers to move freely will help you reach the notes. For example, once you play the fifth-string *D*, release it for the *E*, and then release again for the *G*, etc—instead of stretching for notes, just move your hand. these fingerings are very different from conventional ones; however, the right-hand motion is logical, quick, and effortless.

Arpeggio shapes are probably the most exciting aspect of sweep picking. Once you get a feel for them, they can be played at mind-boggling speeds. Example 39 is a highly useful *Amaj7* arpeggio fingering from which many others can be derived. For example, to convert Example 39 to a dominant 7th pattern, simply lower each G# a half-step. For an *Am7* arpeggio, lower G# a half-step and C# a half-step; see Example 40.

In Example 40 the sweeps cross three and four strings in places. If you count each sweep as a single stroke, then each two-octave arpeggio requires only six pick strokes—in other words, six strokes are used to articulate a total of 16 notes (compared to 16 strokes for 16 notes with conventional alternate picking). The result: Ridiculous speed with minimal right-hand movement.

The simple triadic arpeggio in Example 41—difficult with alternate picking, since it quickly moves across the strings—is easily tackled with sweep picking.

By John Duarte, Jim Ferguson, and Frank Gambale

Example 38.

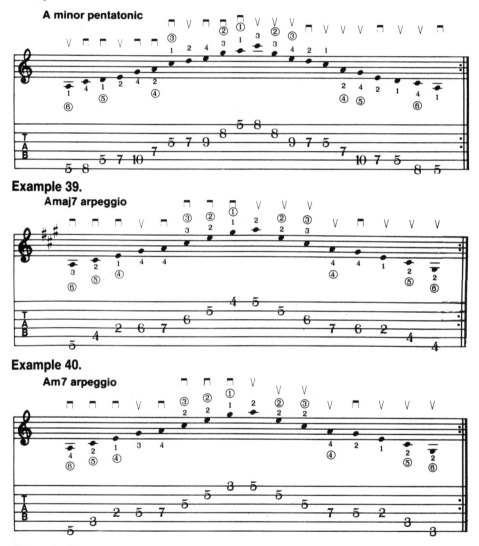

Example 39.

Example 40.

Example 41.

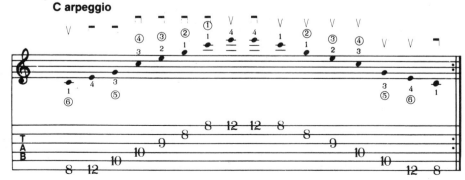

Steve Vai's "Big Trouble" Solo

***Guitar Player**, October 1986.*

The "Big Trouble" solo, from Dave Lee Roth's *Eat 'Em And Smile*, demonstrates Steve Vai's considerable finesse with flashy yet lyrical playing. he recorded the piece with a Charvel Strat-style guitar that's been custom-routed to enable him to pull up on his Floyd Rose tremolo system.

In measure 1 through the first half of bar 4, all the notes with accents ( ) are fingerpicked. Notes with their stems pointing up are plucked with the right-hand finger. For the second half of bar 4, attack the note on the 12th fret of the *B* string, bend it up to the 14th fret before releasing it back to the 12th, and then bend it down with the bar. In measure 6, bring the vibrato bar back to normal position and hammer across the strings. A circle around a note head indicates that the note is fretted with the second finger of the right hand. A diamond around a note indicates it's to be played with your third finger. A diamond-shaped note head indicates a harmonic, achieved by pinching the note with the thumb and pick. After the bend to the *D♯* in the last two beats of measure 10, Steve says, "Return to *C♯* and then bend with the bar down to blubber land."

The special symbols in bars 11 and 12 mean that the notes are approached by a grace note that's created by tapping the vibrato bar in its reversed position, so that the grace note sounds about a third higher than the notes it's approaching. This section features a series of pull-offs, hammers, and "mouse squeaks." "The mouse squeaks are created by the vibrato bar," Vai explains. "If your guitar is set up the same way as mine is, when you pull back hard enough on the bar, the strings fret-out on the highest fret and create a squeak."

By Jas Obrecht

"Big Trouble"

By David Lee Roth and Steve Vai   **Transcribed by Steve Vai**

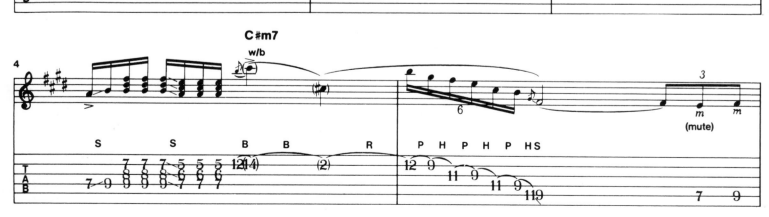

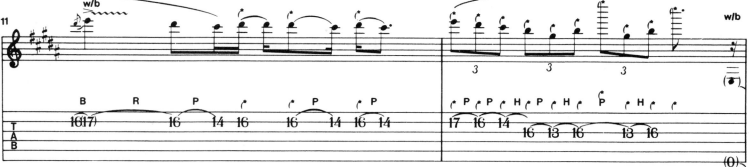

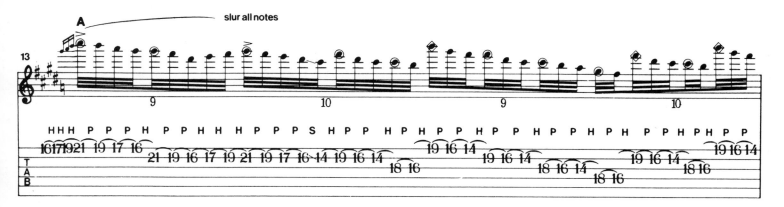

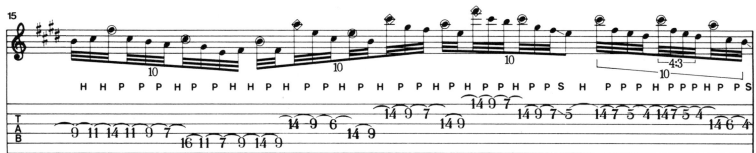

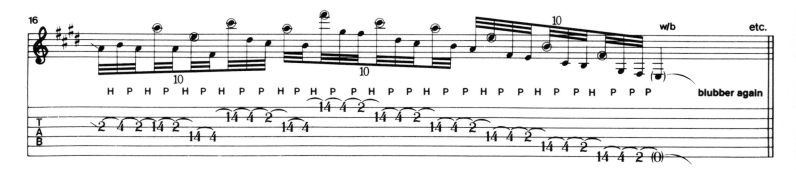

Dokken's "Lightnin' Strikes Again"

Guitar Player, **June 1986.**

Dokken's hard-rocking "Lightnin' Strikes Again" features George Lynch's powerful "call and response" solo. The track in the right side of the stereo spectrum was recorded on a different day than that on the left. "I used completely different sounds and settings for each side," George describes. "The first part that comes in—the thinner one—is my old tobacco-sunburst Fender Strat with no tremolo through a Laney AOR head. Then you hear my tiger-striped Charvel through a Marshall. It's kind of hard to do this solo live because the two parts overlap, but I wanted to do something different."

"Lightnin' Strikes Again" is in the key of *B* minor. The bracketed note values above bars 1 and 19 indicate the duration of the coinciding slides. The solo is basically an overdubbed duet, although a third part appears briefly in bars 29 through 32. George makes extensive use of harmonics created by striking the string simultaneously with the pick and flesh of either the right-hand thumb or first finger; these are indicated in the standard notation by diamond-shaped noteheads. In measures 9 and 10, both the regular note and the harmonic can be heard, while in bars 7 and 8, only the harmonic sounds. George's formidable right-hand picking technique is prominent in bars 20 through 23.

By Jas Obrecht

"Lightnin' Strikes Again"

Words and Music by Don Dokken, George Lynch, Jeff Pilson, and Mick Brown

Transcribed by Mark Small and Tony MacAlpine

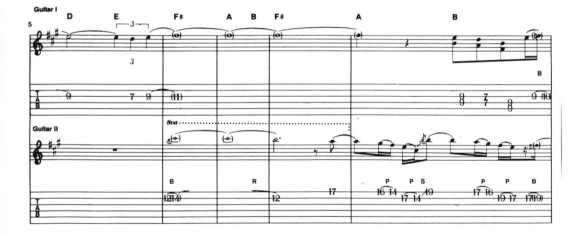

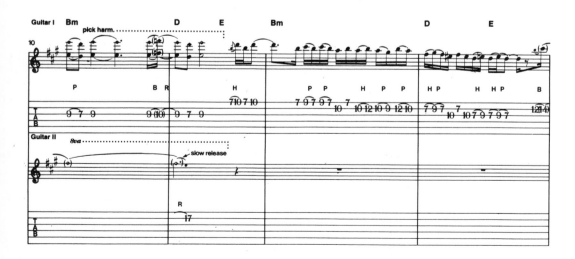

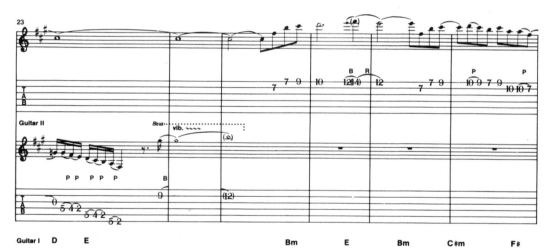

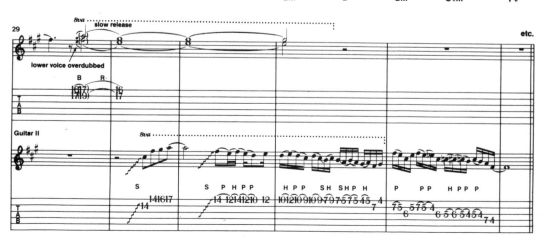

"Flying High Again" A Randy Rhoads Guitar Solo

Guitar Player, **November 1982.**

Many of Randy Rhoads' stylistic traits can be found in his fiery solo in "Flying High Again," a track on Ozzy Osbourne's *Diary Of A Madman* album. Randy uses a repeated motive to get things started in measure 1, and then plays precise ascending and descending scalar passages seasoned with a bit of chromaticism in measures 2 and 3. In measures 4, 6, 8, and 12, his phrases are set off by pauses (held notes, trills) that let the music breathe. Measures 9 through 12 and 13 through 16 are characterized by flashy sounding patterns that work well in sequence.

There are a few technical notes that should be considered when you play this solo. First, measures 1 through 4 and 7 through 14 are transposed down an octave (thus the designation 8va), while measures 5 and 6, as well as 15 and 16, are played as written (loco). At measure 7 the 1st finger bars the *A* and *D* at the 10th fret, while the 4th finger plays the *F#* and *G* on the first string. The pattern in measures 9 through 16 can be played on one string by tapping the first note of the pattern with your index finger or pick, and sounding the other notes with pull-offs and hammer-ons. Left-hand positions are marked as an aid in working through the solo, and double diagonal slashes indicate that you should repeat the preceding sixteenth-note figure.

By Larry Clayton

"Flying High Again"

Chapter 5:
Playing Slide

Slide Guitar Basics: Developing Clean Technique

Guitar Player, March 1984.

Almost every guitarist I have met has been fascinated by the sound of bottleneck slide. However, to many players the techniques involved with this unique style remain a mystery. The following guidelines and exercises are essential in developing the ability to execute clean, accurate, and agile phrases with the slide, and will help you avoid the inefficient method of trial and error.

Why Play Bottleneck?

With the exception of string bending, there is no other way to play the notes "between" the frets. And there is absolutely no other way to get that voice-like singing tone, vibrato, and sustain characteristics of the slide style. Of course, closely linked to these sounds is the kind of bottleneck you use. Although there are acceptable commercial slides available, I prefer ones made from a wine bottle (at least 1/8" thick), because they are *inert* from vibration and have a smooth surface, resulting in a lot less string noise. Although certain players wear their slide on various left-hand fingers, I recommend using the 4th finger. This keeps your other three fingers available for fretted notes and free to dampen string noise (more on this later). Fifth-size Mateus wine bottles make the best slides. The Mateus bottle has one of the few necks long and straight enough (with no flare) to use for playing the guitar. There are also commercial glass slides that work all right, but they aren't as heavy and consequently are harder to use (a heavy slide produces the best tone and is easy to control).

The tricky part about making a good glass slide is cutting the neck off—sometimes you just have to break it free. A glass cutter or a hacksaw can be used to score the neck before breaking, while rough edges can be trimmed with diagonal cutters. (Caution: When cutting glass, always protect your eyes from flying fragments with goggles.) Once the neck is free of the bottle (good luck; be prepared to go through a few fifths), the cut must be ground smooth. Since this process usually takes a few hours, some of you might be able to use the wine. A grinding wheel equipped with a water trough works best for final smoothing, but remember you must use a trough of water to minimize friction and keep the glass from shattering. The important thing is to get the playing edge (where the cut was made) rounded and smooth.

Once you've finished making a satisfactory bottleneck, try it on for size. (I prefer a slide that covers the entire length of the 4th finger.) The bottleneck will be a loose fit, so you''ll have to hold it on by crooking the 4th finger, which helps get the hand into the proper semicircular position for left-hand damping illustrated by Figure 1.

Contacting The Strings

About 80 percent of bottleneck playing uses only the first string. With your hand in a semicircular position, place the slide on the first string, 5th fret, as shown in Figure 2. (Remember, in order to play in tune, you position the bottleneck *directly* over the fret; if you stop to consider how notes are made, you'll see that the frets determine string length and pitch, not your finger.) Once you have located the right note, let the slide contact the string. Don't press down! At the same time, let the flesh of the bottom half of your left-hand 1st finger lightly touch the string behind the slide. This damps the strings and cuts down on extraneous noise, enabling you to get a clean rattle-free tone.

Starting To Play

The first thing to do once you're positioned at the 5th fret is to lazily slide up and down the string. Listen to the sound and maximize its smoothness and tone by adjusting your hand position. It's important to know that your slide hand must be extremely relaxed! Also, take note of how the picking hand influences the tone, depending on how close to the bridge or neck you strike the string. After getting comfortable with this slow up and down sliding, you can start some simple exercises.

Since the material in the following example uses the first string only, it applies to any

Figure 1.

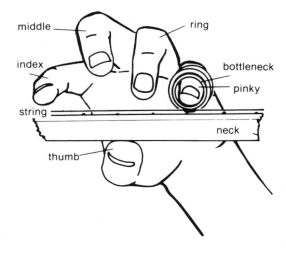

Figure 2.

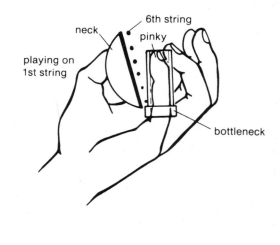

tuning. In addition, I recommend using an instrument strung with medium gauge treble strings, and with action no lower than 1/8" at the 12th fret. Otherwise you will suffer from rattles, missed notes, and a poor "signal-to-noise ratio." Here are some common tunings you might want to experiment with: For electric playing I recommend *A* tuning (*E A E A C# E,* low to high) and *E* tuning (*E B E G# B E,* low to high), because these keys are used extensively for rock and blues. For acoustic playing I recommend *G* tuning (*D G D G B D,* low to high) and *D* tuning (*D A D F# A D,* low to high). Personally, I use the lower tunings, because adjusting strings above concert pitch can put undue tension on an instrument's top and neck. Since open *G* is so widely used and facilitates many of the licks associated with country blues, it generally works best for acoustic music.

From Sounds To Music.

In slide playing, sound and tone are the important things; hot licks come later. The following exercises are designed to develop good tone and *accurate* pitch. Although only the first string (*D*) is used, ultra control can be learned by doing these drills on the remaining five strings as well.

Clean staccato. With a regular beat, play a very short, clean note from the 1st to the 12th fret and back (see Example 1). Leave your 1st finger damping on the string as you lift and return the slide at each fret. The goal is to produce no noise when raising and lowering the bottleneck.

Example 1.

Staccato/open-string combination. Play the same short, clean notes as in the preceding study, but this time lift the slide *and* your damping finger to include the open first string in between each note. Here you must carefully lift and replace the whole hand (slide and damper), while maintaining a semicircular hand position. Work on playing in tune while striving to produce no extraneous noise.

Example 2.

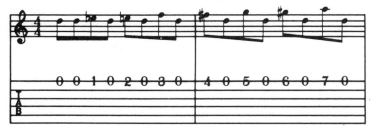 

etc.

Sliding scales. In Example 3, you must try to be clean, controlled, and accurate. Slide up to each note from the designated starting point and hit the next tone perfectly. Although it helps to keep your eye on your left hand, once you master this technique, not looking will really sharpen your ears. A more difficult twist to this exercise is to descend by sliding down to each note:

Example 3.

Strike and slide. Start on *G* at the 5th fret and slide to the next note (Example 4). Pay attention to the time values. This study is also very helpful for timing, pitch, and accuracy.

Example 4.

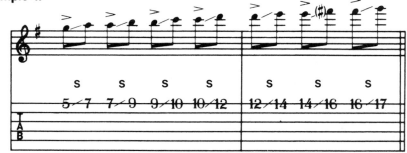

Long jumps. By spelling out the *G7* chord on the first string (Example 5), you learn to leap your whole left hand considerable distances. This is hard to do cleanly and should be practiced two ways: staccato and by sliding up to each tone. The more ways you practice, the more prepared you'll be for various playing situations.

Example 5.

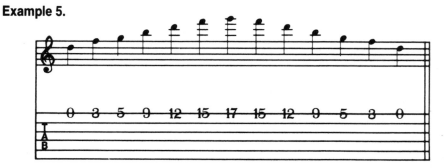

Vibrato Makes The Slide Sing

Vibrato is a shimmering, sustained singing sound characteristic of slide style. The first string is the best place to learn this important technique. Start by positioning the slide at the 5th fret. Vibrato is achieved by rapidly moving the slide back and forth on a note in a left/right motion. However, in practice you don't consciously tell the hand what to do. Let the weight of your hand and slide hang from the left thumb positioned on the back of the neck. This creates a pivot for the left/right movement. The best way to describe how the vibrato motion works is by comparing it to the way you might wiggle a small dish of Jello in somebody's face to make them nervous. The slide hand must be very smooth, slow, relaxed, and with no added weight on the string. Just hang by your thumb and wiggle the slide loose like a goose. This will take some time to develop, so don't lose patience.

The vibrato ranges from the principal note to more than one-half fret below. If it travels above the note, it won't sound right. The speed of the vibrato is variable, but it should definitely be slow enough to be relaxed. If the muscles in the back of your hand are tense, then your playing will sound tense, too. It takes time to get an even, relaxed vibrato, but without it you might as well just be using your left-hand fingers.

What About The Other Strings?

Chords for a basic I IV V blues can easily be played in open G tuning (the same as *A*, only one whole-step lower) by covering three (or more) strings at once. For instance, the first three open strings, as well as the first three strings barred at the 12th fret, yield a G chord (the tonic, or I, chord). The first string is the fifth of the G chord, the second is the third, and the third is the root. At the 5th fret, the same three strings produce a C major (IV), and a D can be played on the 7th fret (V). You can also add the fourth string (fifth of the chord) and the fifth string (root) (see Figure 3). Literally thousands of blues songs are made up of only the I IV V chords.

To play single notes on other strings besides the first, you have to change the angle of the bottleneck (while still damping). Look at Figures 2, 3, and 4 for the three angles that allow you to play on the first string only, more than one string at a time (up to all six), and a single inside string, respectively. Moving back and forth between these positions makes damping tricky, but it's still possible. When sliding on several strings, use the whole length of your left-hand 1st finger for damping. When laying a single inside string use the tip of your 1st finger to damp.

I can't stress enough how important it is to learn the fingerboard well in these tunings. And keep in mind that you can use the 1st (index), 2nd, and 3rd fingers of the left hand to play fretted notes. There are many unique chord voicings that can only be had in these tunings that are certainly worth figuring out. I feel the most interesting open-tuning slide work comes from country blues players such as Robert Johnson, who used fingered notes as much as the slide. Other great bottleneck players you should listen to are Muddy Waters, Tampa Red, Son House, Lowell George, Duane Allman, Bo Weavil Jackson, Kokomo Arnold, and Booker White. If you listen so much that the sound starts coming out your ears, then it's a lot easier to get it out of your hands.

To sum up, let me quickly review the main ideas involved in slide playing: Get your hand position right, making it as relaxed as possible. Play mostly on the first string for the first week or so, trying to develop a fat, smooth, noiseless note with no knocks or rattles. Hang the hand from the thumb on the back of the neck and let the weight of your hand and the slide do the work in producing a vibrato. Don't consciously tell your hand to move back and forth; just wiggle it like Jello. Try every angle of approach to each note. Be able to slide up or down to each note in several different-sounding ways. Keep relaxed in the left hand and remember to play the pitches in tune (over the fret). Don't expect to master this style overnight—there are no shortcuts. And play and listen until slide comes as naturally as singing in the shower.

By Bob Brozman

Figure 3.

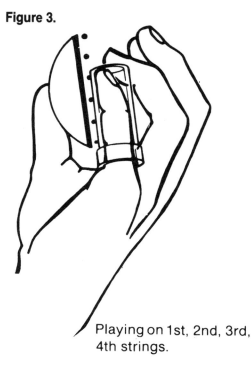

Playing on 1st, 2nd, 3rd, 4th strings.

A SELECTED
BASIC SLIDE DISCOGRAPHY

Individual Artists. Duane Allman: *At Fillmore East,* Capricorn, 2-0131. **Kokomo Arnold and Casey Bill Weldon:** *Bottleneck Guitar Trendsetters Of The 1930s,* Yazoo [c/o Shanachie, Box 810, Newton, NJ 07860], L-1049. **Barbeque Bob:** *Chocolate To The Bone,* Mamlish [Cathedral Station, Box 417, New York, NY 10025], 3808. **Jeff Beck:** *Truth,* Epic, PE-26143. **Ry Cooder:** *Ry Cooder,* Reprise, RPS 6402; *Into The Purple Valley,* Reprise, MS-2052. **Earl Hooker:** *His First And Last Recordings,* Arhoolie [10341 San Pablo Ave., El Cerrito, CA 94530], 1066. **Son House:** *Blind Lemon Jefferson—Son House,* Biograph [16 River St., Chatham, NY 12040], BLP 12040. **Bo Weavil Jackson:** *Bullfrog Blues,* Mamlish, S-3809. **Elmore James:** *One Way Out,* Charly [English import], CRB 1008. **Blind Willie Johnson:** *Blind Willie Johnson,* Folkways [43 W. 61st St., New York, NY 10023], RBF 10. **Robert Johnson:** *King Of The Delta Blues Singers,* Columbia, CL 1654. **Fred McDowell:** *1962—His First Recordings Following Discovery,* Heritage [Box 937, Southampton, PA 18966], HT 302. **Charley Patton:** *Founder Of The Delta Blues,* Yazoo, L-1020. **Bonnie Raitt:** *Bonnie Raitt,* Warner Bros., WBR 1953. **Tampa Red:** *Bottleneck Guitar, 1928-1937.* Yazoo, L-1039. **Keith Richards:** *Sticky Fingers,* Rolling Stone, RLS 39105. **Hound Dog Taylor:** *Natural Boogie,* Alligator [Box 60234, Chicago, Il 60660], 4704. **Muddy Waters:** *McKinley Morganfield: A.K.A. Muddy Waters,* Chess [reissued on Sugar Hill, Box 4040, Duke Station, Durham, NC 27706], 6006. **Booker White:** *Dig Daddy,* Biograph, BOP 12049. **Johnny Winter:** *Johnny Winter,* CBS, 9826.

Anthologies. *Bottleneck Blues Guitar Classics, 1926-1937,* Yazoo, L-1026. *The Voice Of The Blues: Bottleneck Guitar Masterpieces,* Yazoo, L-1046.

By Jim Ferguson

Duane Allman's Slide Style

Guitar Player, **October 1981.**

Duane Allman and slide guitar. To many devotees of Duane's playing with and without the Allman Brothers, the two will forever be inseparable. Duane's slide style had an unmistakable identity that was solely his own, and he possessed one of the most fluid and expressive bottleneck sounds around. Eric Clapton, when asked about his own slide playing in his August '76 *Guitar Player* interview, responded: "I think what really got me interested in it as an electric approach was seeing Duane take it to another place. There were very few people playing electric slide that were doing anything new; it was just Elmore James licks, and everyone knows those. No one was opening it up until Duane showed up and played it a completely different way. That sort of made me think about taking it up."

Well, it's made a lot of others think about doing the same thing, and Duane's playing has helped spawn an entire new generation of slide guitarists, who, since the early '70s, have emulated and imitated his unique style and phrasing. Before we actually go on to playing slide guitar in the Allman style, I feel it is important that we discuss the many facets that go into creating the proper slide sound.

The Slide

Countless objects can be used as slides: Bottle necks, socket wrenches, pill bottles, knives, and brass tubing (my favorite) are just some of the objects that have been seen in the hands of slide players. When choosing a slide, it is important to have something with ample weight so you don't have to press down too hard on the strings, risking a lot of fret and fingerboard noise. In other words, the slide's own weight should help carry it along. Duane almost always used Coricidin bottles, and Lord knows they worked for him. However, the aspiring slide player should be forewarned about a couple of drawbacks to his type of slide. First, it really doesn't have the proper weight to get a truly clean, loud sound (keep in mind that Duane played very loud with the Allman Brothers, mainly utilizing Les Pauls and Marshall amps). Also, this slide was shorter than the width of all six strings, making full chording and lower licks on the slide quite difficult to execute. Last, this type of slide has a closed-off end, and it can get awfully stuffy in there for your finger. You also lose the ability to use the tip of your finger, which, if exposed, can let you know where the end of the slide is for more accurate playing.

Symbol

We'll be using some special symbols to indicate what your slide should do. The symbol in Example 6 means that you slide *up* to that note from approximately two frets below it without giving the original position of the slide any real time value.

Example 7 relates the same thing, only this time you slide *down* to the note from approximately two frets above.

In Example 8, you pick only the first note and then slide to the next, giving both their notated time value.

Example 6.   **Example 7.**   **Example 8.**

Open Tunings

Duane's favorite tunings were open G [*D, G, D, G, B,* and *D,* low to high] and open *E* [*E, B, E, G♯, B, E,* low to high]. These are two of the most popular open tunings for slide guitar, with the latter being more reminiscent of the days of the acoustic Delta blues artists such as Robert Johnson and Son House. Open *E* is more represented in the later playing of Chicago bluesmen such as Elmore James and Tampa Red, who were important in bridging the gap between the rural and the hotter urban styles.

Each tuning has what I call a "box" pattern: an area that, due to the new tuning of the guitar, puts notes of a blues scale within a closer proximity of each other. You'll see what I mean in this example of the open (utilizing open strings) and closed (no open strings) box patterns for an *E* tuning. (Remember that the slide should be positioned directly *over* the guitar's frets, see Example 9.)

Example 9.

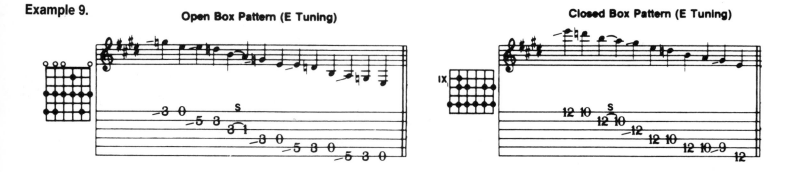

Example 10 shows the two box positions for open *G* tuning. Note how the movement and arrangement of notes are just like *E* tuning, except moved one string higher:

Example 10.

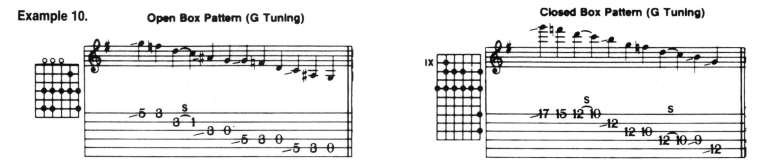

Standard Tuning Slide

Duane played slide in standard tuning quite often. In fact, on some recordings it's a bit hard to decipher any difference between his work in open or standard tunings. One way to be really sure is to listen for any moment where a full *group* of notes are struck that are definitely *not* in standard tuning. For instance, the high *E, B,* and *G♯* of *E* tuning are giveaways, as would be the high *D, B,* and *G* notes for open *G* tuning.

Standard tuning slide is quite difficult and rather limited due to the lack of closer box patterns. Probably the greatest reason for the use of this technique lies in those rare moments when you are called upon to perform both fretted tasks (left-hand fingering) and slide playing in the same song. This situation has occurred more than once for me in the studio, and that's enough for me to know that standard tuning slide should not be taken lightly. Damping strings to prevent any notes other than ones you're sounding to ring out is also crucial to this style, since we are not tuned to any specific chord and therefore must be careful not to sound any extraneous notes.

Example 11 shows the main blues pattern Duane used for standard tuning slide:

Example 11.

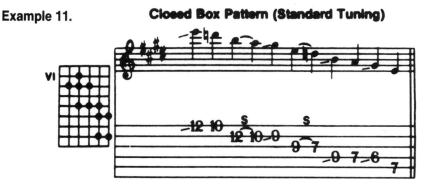

The Right Hand

Fingerpicking is essential to proper slide technique, and even though Duane used a flatpick for his lead playing, he always fingerpicked for slide. I recommended a thumb-and-three-finger approach to slide playing; this style affords you the greatest damping capabilities so important to clean slide playing. Here are two examples of what I mean. In Example 12, your first, second, and third fingers pick the *G, B,* and high *E* strings. When the high *E* string is sounded, the thumb should simultaneously come across and stop the *G* and *B,* leaving only the high *E* to ring. This is an example of how damping is done when a lick moves in the direction of the high *E* string, and how Duane achieved such a smooth, fluid approach to his playing.

Example 12.

If the lick moves in the opposite direction—towards the low *E* string—the fingers that played strings should then serve to stop and rest on the same string, if you wish to damp them out. If the lick continues in the same direction over other strings, you should continue to use your first, second, and third fingers as a *group* for playing and damping, saving your thumb for rhythmic bass notes and damping, Example 13.

Example 13.

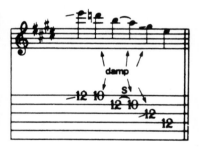

Slide Licks

Next are examples of some slide licks in the Allman style, broken down into the categories of open *E,* open *G,* and standard tunings (Examples 14 and 15). Take note of the similarities between them, as well as their differences. Don't forget to keep the slide straight and damp properly with your picking hand if necessary.

By Arlen Roth

Example 14.

Example 15.

Electric Slide: Muddy Waters' Style

Muddy Waters truly melded the acoustic-oriented Delta style of slide playing into the more modern electric band sound commonly heard on Chicago's South Side. Influenced by Robert Johnson, Muddy's music featured dark, moody vocals and stinging single-note slide phrases played primarily on a Fender Telecaster.

The collective personnel of Waters' bands reads like a who's who of Chicago blues greats, including bassist/songwriter Willie Dixon, harmonica players Little Walter and James Cotton, and pianist Otis Spann. In Muddy's half-century career, he left a virtually unparalleled legacy of blues tunes and performances.

While Muddy used standard tuning almost exclusively in recent years, his slide style was derived from the Delta-based sound of open G tuning [D G D G B D], which he employed during the early part of his career. In order to play in different keys such as A or C, he would merely use a capo. Muddy used a short glass slide worn on his left-hand 4th finger. He would often press down on top of the slide with his 3rd finger for added sustain on the higher frets, and for his patented rapid-fire vibrato.

Open G Tuning

Open G tuning is achieved by lowering the high E string to D tuning the A string down to G (the same pitch as the sixth string, 5th fret), and lowering the sixth string to D (an octave below the open fourth string). (This tuning is not to be confused with the high G tuning used by many Dobro players.) I don't recommend tuning to open A unless you use ultra-light strings and have a guitar with a super-strong neck.

The Slide

I believe in using a relatively heavy slide because you don't have to press down as much and can use lighter strings. In addition, heavy slides produce increased sustain and resonance.

The photo in Figure 5 illustrates the proper position for holding the slide (in this case, a heavy piece of brass tubing). Note that my other fingers lightly touch the strings behind the slide to cut off any overtones that might accidentally occur. And don't use a slide that is overly long, because you won't have as much control.

Guitar Player, **August 1983.**

Figure 5.

Vibrato

Good slide vibrato is created by back and forth motion on either side of the fret you're playing at. Muddy was known for his fast vibrato, which gave his phrases an especially singing quality.

Right-Hand Damping

Whether fingerpicking or not, damping is crucial to accurate slide playing. If a lick moves *toward* the high E string, use your thumb to stop the previous notes from vibrating (see Example 16; the diagonal line leading up to a note head indicates a quick, *upward* slide). When using a slide, remember to position it directly over the fret, and not between frets, as when using your left-hand fingers.

Example 16.

Keep in mind that I recommend a three-finger approach for lead work when fingerpicking. For example, the index, middle, and ring fingers should play the G, B, and E strings, respectively. If a lick moves in the opposite direction of the preceding example, use your right-hand *fingers* to damp with (a diagonal line leading down to a note head indicates a quick downward slide): (Example 17).

Example 17.

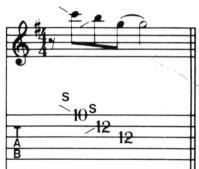

Open G Tuning Box Positions

When it comes to single-note work, there are two box positions (scale patterns) that I like to use. Many of Muddy's licks, including his double-stops, can be played out of these patterns. Example 18 is an open box (using open strings) for G tuning. Be sure to use only as much of the slide as necessary.

Example 18.

Here is a closed box position, which spans a nine-fret distance and enables you to play higher-sounding notes.

Example 19.

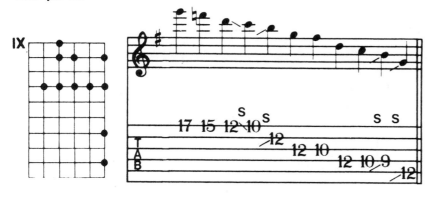

Slide Licks

These licks are in the style of Muddy Waters. Fingerpick as much as possible, and remember to use damping.

By Arlen Roth

Example 20.

= vibrato

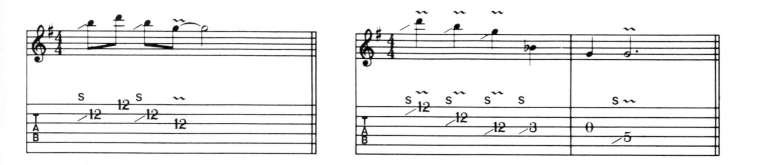

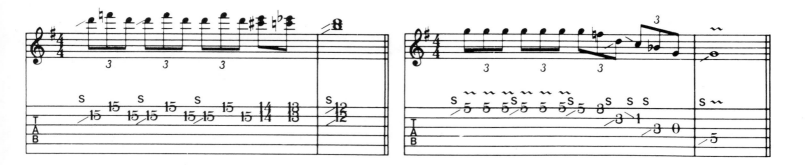

Slide In Standard Tuning

Guitar Player, September 1988.

Slide guitar is one of my favorite topics. Having wirtten my first book on slide way back in 1974 [*Slide Guitar,* Music Sales (24 E. 22nd St., New York, NY 10010)], working with Ralph Macchio on his playing for the movie *Crossroads*, and doing about a million gigs in between, I've come to feel that standard tuning is more limited than open tunings, which facilitate many marvelous things.

But playing slide in standard tuning does have its advantages, so it's well worth exploring. One very important point is that when you're in standard tuning, your right-hand blocking and damping must be flawless, or else you'll end up with an incredible mess and hit discordant extraneous notes. For this reason, it is imperative that you *fingerpick*, which enables you to block and damp with more accuracy. If you want to attempt playing in standard tuning with a pick, the Hot Licks video by former Rolling Stone Mick Taylor features the cleanest and most accurate standard tuning pickstyle slide playing I've ever seen!

Figures 6 and 7 illustrate the positions I recommend for slide fingerpicking technique and pick/fingers technique. Observe how the fingers are poised to play, and how the thumb damps the strings:

Figure 8 shows the proper position of the slide. Notice how the fingers lightly drag behind the slide, damping extraneous sounds, and that the slide is long enough so that the tip of the pinky can sense the end of the slide, which enables you to play single-notes on the lower strings with more accuracy.

Figure 6.

Figure 7.

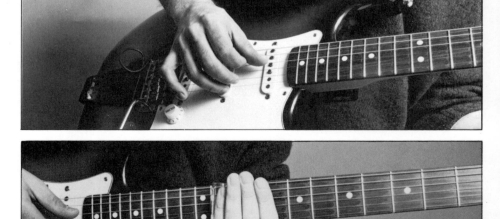

Figure 8.

Here's a blues pentatonic scale fingering designed for slide; (Example 21), it requires that you make full use of your damping abilities. Only when you reach the 9th fret do you have the luxury of a three-note chord to fall back on. On the other hand, open *E* tuning [*E, B, E, G♯, B, E,* low to high], provides *many* possibilities for chordal playing.

Example 21.

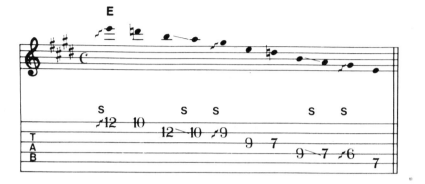

The following licks are from a "box" pattern based around the *E* chord at the 9th fret, which contains a wealth of possibilities, Example 22.

Example 22.

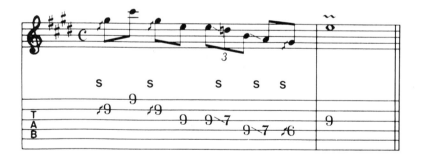

Based on this same "box" pattern, this group of ideas strays from the position a bit more, requiring more sophisticated damping (Example 23). When you take the slide up to the 12th fret, for example, it's very important to lay your right-hand thumb across the bottom strings, in order to prevent unwanted notes:

By Arlen Roth

Example 23.

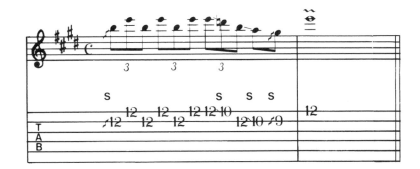

A Guitarist's Introduction To Steel

Guitar Player, June 1987.

Although the pedal steel may look like a strange bird, it's actually a direct descendant of the 6-string guitar. Both instruments have strings that are stretched taut and vibrate between a nut and a bridge, and their *E*-based tunings are similar. The guitar is tuned to the centuries-old Spanish-style 6-string arrangement, while the popular *E9th* pedal steel tuning is built upon an open *E* chord. Now here's the essential difference: Rather than construct chords and single-note runs with fingers pressing down on a fretboard, the steel guitarist frets in a straight line with a metal bar on top of the strings.

To better understand the steeler's thought process, lay your guitar face-up on your lap and tune its open strings to an open *E* chord: *E, B, E, G♯, B, E,* low to high. As you can see, altering only three of your strings will give you the open *E* tuning.

The open strings are now identical to those of the fingered first-position *E* chord in standard tuning. Barring at the 3rd fret gives you a *G* major chord; at the 5th fret you get an *A* chord; at the 8th fret it's a *C* chord; etc.

Here's how you can easily convert your 6-stringer into a makeshift lap steel. [*Ed. Note: The non-pedal lap steel was the forerunner of the pedal-equipped instrument and is still in use, particularly among steelers who play Hawaiian and rock styles; one prominent lap steel player is David Lindley.*] Your local music store will sell you a steel slide bar (I recommend either the Ernie Ball white-end pedal steel bar, the grooved Stevens Dobro-style slide, or any convenient beer bottle). Also, ask your dealer for an extension nut; this miraculous piece of metal fits into place atop your present nut and raises the strings about 3/8″ off the fretboard. Now you can slide without damaging your guitar's precious fretboard.

Hold the bar in your left hand between the thumb and 2nd finger, and place the 1st finger directly on top of the bar. Fan out your 4th and 3rd fingers behind the bar, keeping them flat on the strings. The idea is to prevent unwanted overtones from ringing out behind the bar.

I use National fingerpicks and a plastic Dobro thumbpick on my right hand for playing. This is fairly common, although guitarist/Dobroist James Burton and others have been known to use a flatpick in conjunction with a fingerpick on their middle finger. Find the technique that's comfortable for you. Most players alternate between their thumb and second finger for 75 percent of their single-string attack.

Place your bar at the 3rd fret and strum a *G* chord, and then slide up to the 8th fret for a *C* chord. Try sliding or wiggling the bar just a bit back and forth (parallel to the strings) to add a little vibrato at each chord position. Vibrato lends an irresistible vocal-like quality to the slide tone. To mute a note or chord, simply lift the bar. Use your two fanned-out fingers as an anchor, and they'll damp the note instantly whenever you lift the bar.

Example 24 illustrates some scales related to the key of *E*. I've included both fretted and open-string scale possibilities. Scales are important—they're the musician's alphabet—so practice them often, listening for pitch accuracy and a clean attack.

Example 24.

E major scale

Example 24 (continued).

E major scale

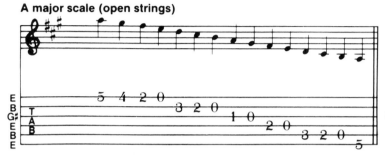

A major scale

A major scale (open strings)

B major scale

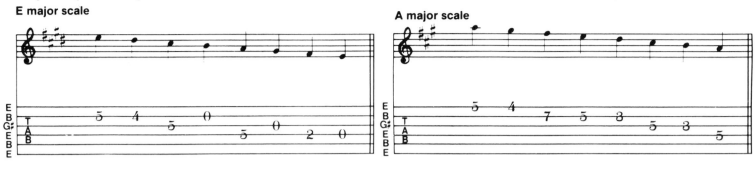

B major scale (open strings)

C♯ natural minor scale

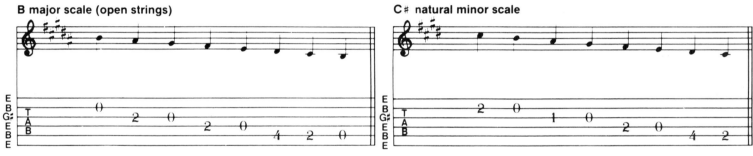

Hot Steel Licks

Now let's play some hot steel licks that'll help develop technique and accuracy. This first one is a lick in *E* combining pull-offs and hammer-ons with open strings (Example 25). Angle the rear of the bar off of the strings, and use only the tip for snappier pull-offs and bounce:

Example 25. E major lick

Here's another lick in *E*, but now we alternate between open strings and notes barred at the 5th fret (Example 26). After fretting the second string, slide the bar towards you and play the open second and third strings, and then move it back to catch the second string again at the 5th fret. This little scale run is tricky at first, but with practice it will blaze through the 55 mph speed limit (be sure to observe the right-hand fingering).

Example 26.

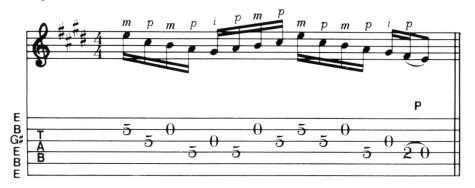

This is a sneaky bar movement passage in *A* that works in every key. Alternate your picking between the thumb and second finger only: (Example 27).

Example 27.

Bar movement lick in A

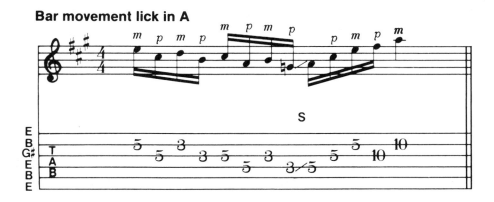

Here's a blues lick in *E* that I love to play. Move that bar fast, and make sure all of the pull-offs are bouncy and crisp (Example 28).

Example 28.
Blues lick in E

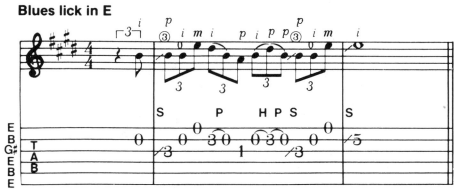

These are some of the basic positons for open *E* tuning. Experiment with them and make up your own licks. You'll have better luck with these exercises on a real steel guitar. Check your local music store or pawnshop for an econo-model lap steel. They have wider necks with clear sightlines, and the pickups are screamers. With a little practice you can join the ranks of crazed steel guitar converts around the world.

By Steve Fishell

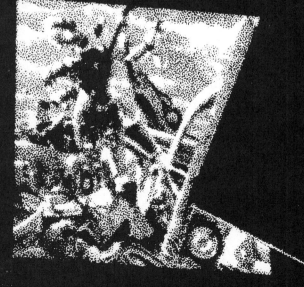

20 Important Rock Albums

Guitar Player, January 1987.

This is not a list of the 20 greatest rock albums ever made, although several surely qualify. Nor are these necessarily the 20 best rock *guitar* albums (for me, Jimi Hendrix' *Electric Ladyland* would top such a list; it's excluded here in favor of his more influential *Are You Experienced*). In some cases, an entire school of playing had to be covered by a single entry. Some of the records cited have sold in the millions; a couple have been scarcely heard. All of them, though, are essential to an understanding of the scope and development of rock guitar.

*   *   *   *

The Sun Sessions
Elvis Presley

"Hold it fellas! That don't *move* me," interrupted Elvis at the start of the "Milkcow Blues" session, Memphis, 1954. "Let's get real, real gone for a change." The sound that followed shook the world. Delivered with reckless abandon and unabashed sexuality, Presley's rockabilly rolled blues, boogie-woogie, and C&W into something vital and irresistible. And almost overnight, it became cool for men to play guitar.

Elvis' sideman, Scotty Moore, became rockabilly's most widely heard lead guitarist. Originally a honky-tonk player from Humbolt, Tennessee, Moore was already a master of the blistering solo and tasty country fill when he recorded *The Sun Sessions* (RCA, AYM1-3893) between 1954 and '56. Given a free hand, he improvised his parts in "Just Because," "Trying To Get To You," and "I Don't Care If The Sun Don't Shine." "A lot of my style was a combination of old blues licks, some Merle Travis, some Chet Atkins, a combination of thumb and finger—just whatever I could make work," he explained. His double-string bends in "Baby, Let's Play House" caused Jimmy Page to take up guitar. Following the Sun sessions, Elvis switched to RCA and cut "Heartbreak Hotel." "After that," Scotty remembered, "it was just like an atomic bomb going off! Nobody even had time to think." Go cats, go.

Ricky Nelson
Ricky Nelson

James Burton joined Ricky Nelson just as the singer was entering his purest rockabilly phase. By the end of 1957, the smiling 17-year-old with the '53 Tele had become rock's most widely recognized sideman, thanks to almost weekly exposure backing Ricky on the hit TV series *The Adventures Of Ozzie And Harriet*. At the time, noted Steve Fishell, "Burton's round, full bass notes and crystaline, hard-driving highs wrote the book for state-of-the-art Fender tone." A master string-bender steeped in country and blues, Burton was one of the first rockers to experiment with light gauges, using banjo strings for his *D, G, B,* and high *E.*

Ricky Nelson (United Artists, UAS-9960) contains the Nelson/Burton classics "Milkcow Blues," "Shirley Lee," the maximum-energy "Believe What You Say," and the impeccably finessed "It's Late" and "Hello Mary Lou." (The 1971 two-disc anthology also includes Ricky's early Verve and Imperial hits "Be Bop Baby," "Waitin' In School," and "Stood Up," with Joe Maphis on guitar.) After quitting Nelson in '65, Burton delved into studio work and became the leader/guitarist of Elvis' comeback band. Today, he's regarded as a country-rock pioneer and the consummate sideman of his generation.

The Great Twenty-Eight
Chuck Berry

In the beginning, there was Chuck Berry. There were no rock and roll blueprints or role models when he cut "Maybeliene" in 1955, just a brown-eyed handsome man from

Tennessee with the imagination to mix blues, '40s swing, and country into something new and exhilarating. His fresh lyrics, strong hooks, and flashy guitarmanship wowed kids then and now—from Keith Richards, Jimi Hendrix, and Eddie Van Halen to anyone who's ever struggled through chapter one of rock guitar. His patented two-string bends and stop-time intro remain rock staples.

While other Chuck Berry compilations are available, *The Great Twenty-Eight* (Chess, CH 8201) is extremely guitar-intensive. All of his big '50s hits are here—"Maybeliene," "Roll Over Beethoven," "School Day," "Rock & Roll Music," "Sweet Little Sixteen," "Johnny B. Goode," "Carol," "Almost Grown," and "Back In The U.S.A."—and "Memphis," "Reelin' And Rockin'," and "Little Queenie." Berry's 1964 comeback hits—"Nadine" and "No Particular Place To Go"—round out the two-record set.

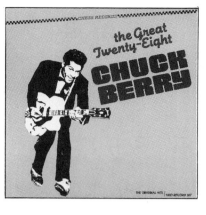

Have 'Twangy' Guitar, Will Travel
Duane Eddy

Credit where credit's due: In 1958 Duane Eddy discovered the commercial potential of rock guitar instrumentals. Foregoing outrageous solos and wild histronics, he brought simple, solid guitar playing right smack centerstage. The cuts on *Have 'Twangy' Guitar, Will Travel* (OutLine Records [Line Music, GMBH, Parkalee 20, D-20000 Hamburg 13, West Germany], OLLP5237 AS) were not only the first to cast the guitar soloist as bandleader/rock star, but they also popularized a very specific sound. As heard in "Rebel 'Rouse," "Ram Rod," "Detour," and "Cannon Ball," Duane's twangy tone was a combination of melodies picked on his Gretsch hollowbody's bass strings, gentle whammy shakes, heavy amp tremolo and reverb, and echo caused by miking a speaker in an empty 500-gallon water tank. Steve Douglas' smoky sax provided a perfect foil.

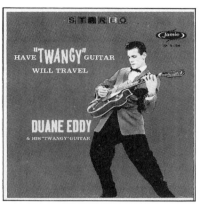

By the time his career began to ebb in 1963, Duane had sold 12 million records and had been on the charts more than any other rock instrumentalist—a record that still holds. In his wake followed a spate of guitar bands. The Ventures' Bob Bogle contended, "Duane's about the only act whom I'd have no qualms about opening for."

Walk—Don't Run
The Ventures

The album that launched a thousand bands. Back in my neighborhood, it was an exciting—*monumental*—event when someone finally mastered the riff of "The Switch," the melody of "Walk—Don't Run." The quintessential '60s guitar band, the Ventures specialized in instrumentals with catchy melodies and cool chord changes that were simple enough to copy. Sure, even moms and pops dug dream lovers' ballads such as "Sleep Walk," but this Seattle quartet could *rock*. And how! All in their early twenties when they cut 1960's *Walk—Don't Run* (Dolton, BST 9003; out of print), Bob Bogle and Don Wilson handled the lead and rhythm guitar parts, respectively; Nokie Edwards, later their lead player, concentrated on bass.

"The Switch" bristled with wicked guitar rhythms and fiery solos. The wang-bar inflections and muted picking of "Morgen" presaged the surf phenomenon, which was still a couple of years away. The reverb-laden melody lines of "Walk—Don't Run" were pure dynamite. Inspired by Chet Atkins and Duane Eddy, the Ventures, in turn, influenced countless others with this rock guitar primer.

Beggars Banquet
The Rolling Stones

Seldom has an album been identified so closely with the politics of the day. *Beggars Banquet* (London, PS-539) was written and recorded during two months of the politically volatile spring of 1968, and "violence" was the common catchword of its first reviews. Sure enough, "Street Fighting Man" is a mighty potent call to arms. Musically, the album showcases Keith Richards' virtuosity. His strummed, open-tuned acoustic guitar rhythms create immense power and urgency; the band follows his every innuendo. At his best, he fuses lead and rhythm into a single voice—witness "Street Fighting Man," "Parachute Woman," or "Stray Cat Blues." Roots country blues licks and poignant slide drive "No Expectations," while "Prodigal Son" covers a Robert Wilkins country blues classic. Flatpicked, "Der Doctor" parodies American C&W. The electric guitar surfaces most often for accents—piercing leads in "Sympathy For The Devil," wavering slide in "Jig-Saw Puzzle" and "Salt Of The Earth." And, there's even some sitar.

Beatles VI
The Beatles

While many Beatles releases can be counted as essential guitar albums, *Beatles VI* (Capitol, ST 2358) was chosen for several reasons. Most important, it highlights the band's early reliance on the acoustic guitar as a principal rhythm instrument. George Harrison and John Lennon collaborate on several unison parts, playing either acoustic guitar and electric 12-string (George is pictured on the back holding a Rickenbacker) or two electrics. They pay homage to their roots in American rock and roll, rockabilly, and country with the Chet Atkins-inspired country fingerpicking of "I Don't Want To Spoil The Party" and covers of "Kansas City" and Buddy Holly's "Words Of Love." The raucous "Dizzy Miss Lizzy" and "Bad Boy" are classic examples of primal Lennon vocals. The band's experimental side surfaces in the volume swells of "Yes It Is."

Having A Rave Up With The Yardbirds
The Yardbirds

"What's a rave up?" asks the liner notes. "It's the sound of the future—the Yardbirds' sound of the future!" Truer words were never written. On his recording debut, Jeff Beck emerged as a full-fledged guitar hero—menacing, flamboyant, ungodly energetic—and laid down the shapes of things to come. Side one, all studio tracks, concerns us most. Jeff pioneered the use of fuzz in "You're A Better Man Than I," "Heart Full Of Soul," and other tunes. His volume-swell whistles launched "Train Kept A-Rollin'," his slide lines fueled "Evil Hearted You." His solo climax in "I'm A Man" virtually exploded off the fingerboard in a frenzy of rhythm. Beck stepped out furthest in "Heart Full Of Soul," simulating a sitar; it paid off with one of the classic hits of the psychedelic era.

Side two—the "live" side—is from *Five Live Yardbirds* (Charly, CR 30173) and features Eric Clapton, who's mostly relegated to repeated riffs and chugging rhythms until the propulsive rave-up of "Here 'Tis." Today, the Yardbirds' second American album sounds something like the ultimate garage band meets an end-of-the-world guitarist. For a while in '65, though, *Having A Rave Up With The Yardbirds* (Epic, LN 24177) contained rock's freshest, most vital guitar playing.

Are You Experienced
Jimi Hendrix Experience

Fiery, magnificent, and tender, *Are You Experienced* (Reprise, RS 6261) is the most revolutionary debut album in rock guitar history. Released in June 1967, it made Jimi Hendrix a worldwide sensation and forever expanded the instrument's range. While others had experimented with feedback, distortion, massive volume, wah-wah, octave doubling, whammy, and other effects, Hendrix was the first to harness them enough to create music both extraordinarily imaginative and enduring.

Hendrix' debut displayed almost the full breadth of his talents. Its multi-layered arrangements, ping-ponging production, and approach to tones, chord voicings, and solos were unlike any in rock. The title track began with *backwards* guitar. Fuzzed-out hits, "Purple Haze" and "Foxey Lady" seemed to summarize the summer of '67. With guitar-created wind effects, horse neighs, and amazing feedback, "Third Stone From The Sun" took psychedelic guitar to its furthest extremes. Jimi taps his Curtis Mayfield / R&B roots for the sheer poetry of "The Wind Cries Mary." Excellent on compact disc, *Are You Experienced* is as stunning today as two decades ago.

Led Zeppelin II
Led Zeppelin

"Jimmy Page's solos are fantastic," insisted Carlos Santana, "but it's his sense of composition that has everybody down. He carries a sense of total vision. To me, he's the one who took over what Jimi was doing—you know, that sense of enormous rock and roll, a Stravinsky-type thing." Nowhere is Page's vision more total, his sensibilities more enormous, than on 1969's *Led Zeppelin II* (Atlantic, SD 8236). Many players—Steve Morse among them—consider this to be *the* album that established the formula for heavy metal guitar. Great arrangements abound, and the sound and feel of Page's guitar—especially in "Whole Lotta Love"—have been much imitated. Released in October '68, the album became the fastest-selling in Atlantic history, averaging sales of more than 100,000 copies a *week* through the summer of 1970.

Live At Leeds
The Who

Onstage with the Who, Pete Townshend personified the concept of finesse under pressure. Sans studio overdubbing, he integrated rhythm and lead into a passionate style that's complete unto itself. His magnificent performance in the 14-minute "My Generation" should live as long as rock and roll itself. Alternately subtle and angry, knuckle-busting windmill chords give way to blazing single-line assaults, tender arpeggios, and simultaneous bass and guitar soloing. The band's readings of jazz pianist Mose Alison's "Young Man Blues," Eddie Cochran's "Summertime Blues," and Johnny Kidd & The Pirates' "Shakin' All Over" reach heights that the composers could never have imagined. Much solo credit goes to John Entwistle, who almost singlehandedly redefined the bass' potential in a concert setting. Clearly among rock's foremost live albums, 1970's *Live At Leeds* (MCA, 3023) was followed by *Who's Next* (MCA, 1691), arguably the band's best studio effort.

Wheels Of Fire
Cream

Brilliant soloists all, Eric Clapton, Jack Bruce, and drummer Ginger Baker conjured their most astonishing musical alchemy on *Wheels Of Fire* (RSO, 2-3802). The album is divided into two discs: "In The Studio" and "Live At The Fillmore." For the studio set, Eric laced "Born Under A Bad Sign" and "Sitting On Top Of The World" with note-perfect blues, and explored the boundaries of wah-wah rhythms and feedback doubling in "White Room." He strummed "As You Said" and "Deserted Cities Of The Heart" on acoustic. There are many instances of guitar overdubs by a single guitarist, which were much rarer in 1968 than today. Two Fillmore cuts document the live Cream at its peak. Classic Clapton, the "Crossroads" solo alone is worth the price of admission. At 16:44 minutes, "Spoonful" provides the most revealing example of Cream's inner workings. Eric's tone—the raw crunch of a Gibson SG/Les Paul through a Marshall stack—quickly became rock's most sought-after guitar sound. This LP is best heard on compact disc or Mobile Fidelity's excellent Original Master Recording pressings.

Van Halen
Van Halen

Van Halen (Warner Bros. BSK 3075) had more impact on rock guitarists than any release since *Are You Experienced*. Using a Strat-style guitar he "slapped together" himself, 20-year-old Eddie Van Halen unleashed fire-breathing sounds that seemed to leap off the vinyl. He executed solos with dazzling skill, took a kamikaze approach to the whammy bar and effects devices, and crammed growls, shrieks, and explosions into every available crevice. Underlying all the fury was a strong sense of composition and the melodic and rhythmic sensitivity of a classically trained pianist. Eddie's "Eruption," the most famous heavy metal solo blitz of all, introduced his much-imitated fingertapping technique. (Jimmy Webster had developed an advanced tapping style decades before, but Van Halen was the first major-league rocker to make it his stylistic cornerstone.) Eddie's impact in 1978 was immediate, his rise to fame meteoric. By the decade's end, fingertapped guitar solos were a garage band staple. But as much as his techniques or wild energy, it's Eddie's personality—his sense of humor—that ranks him among rock's most distinctive players.

Ghost In The Machine
The Police

The late '70s and early '80s brought the rise of the *textural* school of guitar playing. Long, drawn-out solos and flash blitzes gave way to subtle rhythms, rich tones, and short fills. While The Edge of U2, Rush's Alex Lifeson, and Adrian Belew all made the school's honor role, Andy Summers became its dean with the release of 1983's *Ghost In The Machine* (A&M, SP-3730). A master of tasteful understatement and sonic effects, he sends a rainbow swath of sound swirling through Stewart Copeland's drumming and Sting's bass work. Most guitar parts are intricate, provocative, and airy. "Secret Journey" features massive guitar synthesizer tones, while blazing fills riddle "Demolition Man." "One World" reprises the reggae-scratch rhythms that characterize earlier Police albums. Summers' "Omegaman" solo is charged with emotion.

The Allman Brothers Band At Fillmore East
Allman Brothers Band

My choice for rock's greatest live album, *The Allman Brothers Band At Fillmore East* (Capicorn, CPN-2-0131) casts an innovative group at its kinetic peak. Without effects or studio gimmicks, Duane Allman and Dickey Betts roar to life with incredible power and emotion. There are no wasted notes, no pointless jams. In the process, they inaugurated a trend for bands having two guitarists who play melodic—but not always predictable—harmonies. For many, it was the most original, exciting guitar playing of the early '70s.

This album and live cuts on *Eat A Peach* and *Duane Allman: An Anthology* were all cut on March 12 and 13, 1971. Duane's performances in "Statesboro Blues," "Done Somebody Wrong," and other tracks set a still-unsurpassed standard for slide guitar. He and Dickey gave commanding blues performances in "You Don't Love Me" and "Stormy Monday," and created groundbreaking unison parts in other songs. Allman's no-holds-barred climax of "In Memory Of Elizabeth Reed" may be his brightest moment. Excellent on compact disc.

Blow By Blow
Jeff Beck

Jeff Beck made his chanciest career move when he abandoned blues-based rock to immerse himself in jazz-rock fusion. When he announced his plans to cut an album in late '74, observers considered the project risky, at best. Within weeks of its release, though, *Blow By Blow* (Epic, PE 33409) had become a hit—an astonishing feat for an instrumental rock album. Producing was George Martin, who had worked on virtually every Beatles recording. Beck and sidemen—bassist Phil Chen, keyboardist Max Middleton, and drummer Richard Bailey—proved virtuosic on every track. Intricate rhythms and overdubs abound, and Beck even explores the role his guitar could play with an orchetra. Dedicated to guitarist Roy Buchanan, Jeff's cover of "'Cause We've Ended As Lovers" stands among his most lyrical performances. Afterwards, Beck shared billings with the Mahavishnu Orchestra and returned to funk-fusion on 1976's *Wired* (Epic, PE-33849).

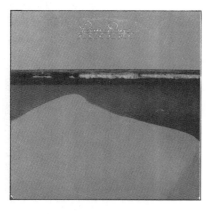

What If
Dixie Dregs

Truly a guitarist's guitarist, Steve Morse proved his astounding mastery of composition and technqiue on 1978's *What If* (Capricorn, CPN 0203). Writing nearly every note for every instrument, he orchestrated his musicians into a top-flight fusion *band* rather than a collection of soloists. His own playing mixes soaring jazz-rock, traditional folk, chicken-scratch country, Baroque/classical, heavy metal riffs, and free-form synth explorations. Culling myriad tones from his multi-pickup Telecaster and advanced effects setup, Steve sings and singes, lulls and captivates. Every note truly counts.

Morse aims true when doubling lines with other instruments. "Gina Lola Breakdown" and "Ice Cakes" exemplify worldclass chicken picking. Violin and classical guitar reel to a jig beat in the "Little Kids" duet. Punctuated by volume swells, chord melodies, and breakneck fusion passages, the bittersweet "Odyssey" counts among his most memorable works. Although this LP has long been out of print, used copies are well worth searching out. Steve went on to expand his range on other projects with the Dregs and Steve Morse Band, but the foundation's all here.

Layla
Derek & The Dominos

Eric Clapton's finest work and one of the greatest albums in rock history. His vocals have seldom been as impassioned, his multi-track guitar layering and straight soloing as stunning. The cuts are pressed in the order they were recorded during October 1970. Clapton alone plays guitar on "I Looked Away," "Bell Bottom Blues," and the densely textured "Keep On Growing." Duane Allman, the brilliant slide and lead guitarist for the Allman Brothers Band, was then brought in. The pairing proved to be the meeting of two kindred minds and 20 amazing fingers, with the guitarists rapidly challenging each other to new heights.

Duane blazes amazing slide trails through "Key To The Highway," "Nobody Knows You When You're Down And Out," "It's Too Late," and "Have You Ever Loved A Woman." Their exchanges grow white-hot by the time of the simultaneous leads in "Why Does Love Got To Be So Sad?" Eric pours his soul into "Have You Ever Loved A Woman," blasting volleys of perfect blues between anguished vocals. Both Clapton and Allman track slide on the album's masterpiece, "Layla." The only outtake released from *Layla* (Atco, SD2-704) sessions is the acoustic guitar duet "Mean Old World" on *Duane Allman: An Anthology* (Capricorn, 0108). Afterwards, Clapton credited Allman with renewing his interest in slide guitar.

Metal Fatigue
Allan Holdsworth With I.O.U.

While Allan Holdsworth soloed mightily on past projects with Soft Machine, U.K., and others, 1985's *Metal Fatigue* (Enigma, 72002-4) gives the best representation of his groundbreaking chordal approach and expansive tonal palette. Drawing on his sophisticated musicality, tremendous left-hand reach, and ultra-lyrical whammy touch, he forges a unique jazz-rock style. "Devil Take The Hindmost" juxtaposes singing legato lines with fast, flashy passages, while "The Un-Merry-Go-Round" is punctuated with emotive soprano cries. The guitarist unleashes startling new sounds on "Home," "Panic Station," and the title track. Producing himself, Allan achieves a superb sound on all tracks. Soon after *Metal Fatigue's* release, Holdsworth embarked on his celebrated exploration of guitar synthesis.

The Royal Scam
Steely Dan

The jazziest pop-rock band of the '70s, Steely Dan issued its funk-oriented *The Royal Scam* (ABC, ABCS 931) in 1976. While the LP features guitarists Dean Parks, Dennis Dias, Elliot Randall, and Walter Becker, Larry Carlton emerged as the man with the golden touch. The perfect foil for Donald Fagen's jazz-derived harmonies and cryptic lyrics, he delivered confident, finesse-packed solos in "Kid Charlemagne," "Don't Take Me Alive," "The Royal Scam," and "Everything You Did." His superb tone had a massive effect on the studio scene, sending players in New York, Hollywood, and points in between scurrying to music stores for Gibson ES-335s, Mesa/Boogie amps, and volume pedals. The album was certified gold by September 1976, with singles "The Fez" and "Kid Charlemagne" breaking into the Top 100. Already a veteran of the Jazz Crusaders, Carlton went on to forge a successful solo career.

By Jas Obrecht

About The Authors

Larry Clayton is a freelance writer and music editor who's work has appeared in *Guitar Player* and other music publications.

Bruce Bergman is a New York attorney and leading club-date rock guitarist and bassist. He is also the author of *How To Make Money Playing Rock Guitar*, from which his article in this book is excerpted.

Bob Brozman is a bottleneck blues and Hawaiian steel performer and instructor who has recorded solo albums on the Kicking Mule label.

Rick Derringer first topped the charts in the mid '60s with his hit "Hang On Sloopy" with the McCoys. His collaborations with Johnny and Edgar Winter, Steely Dan, Ted Nugent, Todd Rudgren, and Meat Loaf have established him as a versatile and imaginative performer.

John Duarte is one of the world's foremost composers for classical guitar. His works have been performed by such greats as Andres Segovia and Alexander Lagoya. He is also a columnist for *Guitar Player*.

Rik Emmett is the guitarist/singer/composer for the Canadian rock trio Triumph.

Jim Ferguson is an associate editor for *Guitar Player* magazine.

Steve Fishell is a mainstay of Emmylou Harris' Hot Band, and he's a featured pedal steel guitarist on the top-selling Harris/Linda Ronstadt/Dolly Parton *Trio* album.

Frank Gambale is a fusion wizard who has played with bassist Jeff Berlin and violinist Jean Luc Ponty. Currently he is a member of Chick Corea's Elektric Band. His solo album debut, *Brave New Guitar*, was released in 1986, and he is featured on Corea's LP *Light Years*.

Brad Gillis is the guitarist for the rock group Night Ranger. He boasts a platinum album for Ozzy Osbourne's million-selling *Speak Of The Devil*, as well as gold and platinum awards for Night Ranger's *Dawn Patrol*, *Midnight Madness*, and *7 Wishes*.

Steve Morse recorded a half-dozen albums with the Dixie Dregs (later known as the Dregs), and then unveiled the Steve Morse Band. He has won five consecutive *Guitar Player* Readers Polls, and he's currently working with the rock group Kansas.

Jas Obrecht is an associate editor for *Guitar Player* magazine.

Lee Ritenour was for five years one of Hollywood's premier studio guitarists, appearing on more than 200 albums and some of the best-selling soundtracks in history (Saturday Night Fever and Grease). For the past few years he has concentrated on a performing career and has recorded a number of successful albums with his own band.

Arlen Roth is a solo recording artist who has also backed artists including Simon & Garfunkel and Phoebe Snow. He founded the Hot Licks audio and video cassette instructional series.

Johnny Smith has been a valuable contributor to *Guitar Player* for many years. He won numerous polls as a jazz soloist and became the namesake of one of Gibson's elegant arch-top guitars. For the past 30 years he has owned and operated the Johnny Smith Music Center in Colorado Springs, Colorado, where he repairs guitars.

From The *Guitar Player* Magazine Basic Library:

BASIC GUITAR (Revised)
Edited by Helen Casabona, Foreword by Les Paul
A completely updated edition of the most comprehensive, single-volume introduction to the technique and art of playing guitar. From the pages of *Guitar Player* magazine.
ISBN 0-88188-910-5 $14.95

GUITAR SYNTH AND MIDI
Edited by Bradley Wait
Expand your sounds and create options with guitar synthesis. This introductory book takes you from basic concepts through advanced applications of this brave new world. From the pages of *Guitar Player* magazine.
ISBN 0-88188-593-2 $14.95

ELECTRIC BASS GUITAR (Revised)
Edited by Andy Doerschuk
All you'll need to know about getting started, reading music, practicing, techniques, soloing, progressions, patterns, bass lines, scales, chords, and ways to modify your instrument. Filled with productive lessons and musical examples, all from the pages of *Guitar Player* and *Bass Player* magazines.
ISBN 0-88188-907-5 $14.95

Also from GPI Books:

MASTERS OF HEAVY METAL
Edited by Jas Obrecht
"Goes to the eye of the hurricane," (Portland, Oregonian). "Fascinating!" (Newark Star Ledger). For fans and players of the immensely powerful, hugely popular, hard-core rock and roll style: intense, high-energy, guitar-dominated. Including serious, informative interviews with Jimi Hendrix, Eddie Van Halen, Jimmy Page, Randy Rhoads, Judas Priest, the Scorpions, and others. Profusely illustrated.
ISBN 0-688-02937-X $12.95

THE BIG BOOK OF BLUEGRASS
Edited by Marilyn Kochman, Foreword by Earl Scruggs
Bill Monroe, Lester Flatt, Earl Scruggs, David Grisman, Ricky Skaggs, and other popular bluegrass artists offer practical tips on playing, with note-by-note musical examples, plus valuable advice on technique and performance. The history, the greatest players, the genuine art of this authentic American commercial country folk music, more popular than ever today. Over 100 rare photos and over 50 favorite songs.
ISBN 0-688-02942-6 $12.95

GUITAR GEAR
Edited by John Brosh
A definitive guide to the instruments, accessories, gadgets, and electronic devices; the tremendous variety of both basic and sophisticated equipment that has become so crucial to the creative fulfillment of today's guitar player—how it works, how it's made, how to choose what's right for you.
ISBN 0-688-03108-0 $15.95

NEW DIRECTIONS IN MODERN GUITAR
Edited by Helen Casabona
A wealth of insight into the styles and techniques of guitarists who have moved into the vanguard of contemporary music. Artists such as Adrian Belew, Robert Fripp, Stanley Jordan, acoustic wizard Michael Hedges, and bassist Jaco Pastorius are covered in depth—with interviews, instructive musical examples, and an analysis of their playing and equipment
ISBN 0-88188-423-5 $14.95

THE GUITAR PLAYER BOOK
By the Editors of *Guitar Player* Magazine
The most comprehensive book on guitar ever produced, from the pages of America's foremost magazine for professional and amateur guitarists. Any style, any level, whether player or fan—this is the book. Includes definitive articles on all the important artists who have given the guitar its life and expression, plus design, instructions, equipment, accessories, and technique.
ISBN 0-394-62490-4 $11.95

NEW AGE MUSICIANS
Edited by Judie Eremo
The philosophy and techniques of this influential instrument style. Interviews with the foremost visionaries, including Kitaro, Will Ackerman, George Winston, and Michael Hedges. From the pages of *Guitar Player*, *Keyboard*, and *Frets* magazines.
ISBN 0-88188-909-1 $14.95

BEGINNING SYNTHESIZER
A step-by-step guide to understanding and playing synthesizers with discussions of how to use and edit presets and performance controls. A comprehensive, easy-to-understand, musical approach, with hands-on lessons in a variety of styles, including rock, pop, classical, jazz, techno-pop, blues, and more.
ISBN 0-88284-353-2 $12.95   From Alfred Publishing. (Item Number 2606).